Contents

Key Stage 1

Key Stages 1&2

Key Stages 2

Introduction

This collection of reproductions of works of art has been chosen carefully to provide you and your school with a range of reference material that you can use with children in Key Stages 1 and 2. The National Curriculum in Art requires that children should become familiar with the work of artists, craftworkers and designers who have made work at different times and in different cultures (see page 3).

Using works of art with children has several purposes:
- it helps them to understand and evaluate their own making;
- it helps them to make positive connections between their own work and that of other artists and designers;
- it extends their knowledge about the place of art in the wider community and in different cultures.

You will find detailed guidance about ways in which you can use works of art with children in *Knowledge and Understanding in Art*.

CHOICE OF WORK

The choice of work in this collection obviously reflects the authors' interests and contains many works that we have used successfully in our work with children and in in-service training with primary school teachers. Choosing 24 works from the whole history of Art and Design presented us with many difficult and conflicting decisions! However, we hope that presenting you with this range of work will help you to recognise what a rich variety of resource material is available to you in the work of artists and designers.

The collection ranges in time from the 8th century Book of Kells (card 17) to work made by artists in the 1960s and 1970s. It includes work from a wide range of countries and cultures and by both male and female artists. It includes work made using a variety of materials and processes and to satisfy different social functions and purposes.

ACCESS AND AVAILABILITY

The bulk of the work in this collection has been chosen because it is easily accessible and is by artists whose work is familiar. Most of the work is in collections in the United Kingdom and this will mean that children in some areas will be able to visit local galleries and museums and see the original work. However good a reproduction is of a work of art it cannot compare with the impact of its original.

Much of the work in this collection is also available on postcards; so you could buy sets of postcards to match the reproductions. This would help you to organise follow-up work more effectively: you can use the reproductions to focus class discussion and the children can have their own 'postcard' version for closer and individual study.

You will be able to find supporting books about the various artists' work through your local library service. Then you can show pupils other examples of the artist's work.

The collection contains only two reproductions of work in three dimensions: Dame Elisabeth Frink's sculpture 'Goggle Head' (card 18) and a Yoruba carving from Nigeria (card 8). This is because it is very difficult to do justice to a work in three dimensions in a two-dimensional photograph. In *Knowledge and Understanding in Art* you will find one very good example of the way that a teacher used a collection of photographs of Rodin's 'The Burghers of Calais' to generate exciting three-dimensional work with children.

USING THE COLLECTION

The collection of works is arranged in sequence. Numbers 1–6 are recommended for use in Key Stage 1; numbers 7–12 for use in Key Stages 1 or 2; and numbers 13–24 for use in Key Stage 2. They are also presented in approximate order of complexity: the earlier works have a strong storytelling bias appropriate to Key Stage 1; the later works are more complex and demanding and are for use with older children.

The sequence is not arbitrary! You will find that many of these works can be used equally successfully with children of different ages. Your own interest in particular works will have an important bearing upon how successfully you use them with children.

Because all the reproductions are approximately the same size it is important to note the real scale of the work. Some of them are very big paintings; for example, Uccello's 'The Rout of San Romano' (card 21) and Hockney's 'Mr and Mrs Clark and Percy' (card 12). You will need to help the children to understand their scale by getting them to measure out how large they are on the floor or on a wall of the classroom.

THE FRAMEWORK

About the artist

This section provides a brief account of the artist's life and work. It is intended to help you place the artist's work in context for the children so that they know something about the artists, when and how they lived, and what kind of people they were. (Words in **bold** are explained in the Glossary.)

About this work

This section will give you information about the work itself: how and why it was made, for what purpose and how it relates to other work made by the artist.

Discussion points

This section is also printed on the reverse of the card showing the reproduction of the work, so that it can act as a prompt for you as you present the work to the children. The text in this section consists of useful information and questions that you can ask the children to help them focus into what the work is about and how it is made. It is intended to generate discussion about the work and lead to other questions. Some of the questions lead into simple tests that will help the children 'see' the work more clearly.

Sometimes the children will be invited to make comparisons between different works in the collection in order that they might see how artists working in different times or cultures respond to the same subject matter. For example, the comparison between the double portraits made by Thomas Gainsborough in the 18th century (card 19) and by David Hockney in the 20th century (card 12).

On card 5, the text in this section is entitled THINGS TO DO as the copy refers to simple tasks, rather than questions.

Activities

These are examples of the many different kinds of activities that might be undertaken with children in response to the particular work of art. Some of them will suggest other activities and the children themselves will have interesting ideas about how they might respond practically and imaginatively to the work.

Some of the activities are to do with investigating and seeking out important elements in the work, such as detail and colour. Other activities will help the children to understand how the artist has made the work and to compare one artist's methods with another's.

All the activities lead on to helping the children to make practical responses to artists' work through creating work themselves which explores similar challenges, problems and subject matter.

Evaluation

Questions are presented to help you and the children reflect upon what understanding has been achieved through the study of this work.

SOME STARTING POINTS FOR USING WORKS OF ART

Although there are detailed suggestions for those activities that you might undertake with children in response to each of the works of art in this pack, you may find the following general information useful to your thinking about planning for work in critical studies.

● Always try to begin any work with opportunities for group discussion between children. They will respond better to open discussion about works of art if they first share their interest and responses within smaller, less threatening groups.

● Don't embark upon any work in using works of art without sufficient resources to generate discussion across a full class group.

● Where necessary, use simple worksheets or questionnaires to help children focus upon information and detail within the work.

● Use combinations of focusing devices, e.g. viewfinders and magnifying glasses, to help children to 'see' the work. This is particularly important when studying very detailed or complicated work.

Liking and disliking

Liking a work can be as dismissive as disliking it. Try to find ways to encourage positive reasons from the children for liking and disliking.

● Present the group with six pictures that are very different in their subject matter (their content). Ask them to choose the two they like best and the two they dislike most, with the proviso that they state at least three different reasons for liking and disliking each work. Ask the group to come to some consensus about why some work is more favoured than others.

● Present the group with three paintings which are similar in subject matter but which are very differently painted; e.g. the married couples in 'Mr and Mrs Andrews' (card 10), 'The Last of England' (15), and 'Mr and Mrs Clark and Percy' (12). Establish, through discussion, which work is most admired and why:
  – Which is the most realistic?
  – Which has the nicest colours?
  – Which would they most like to own?
  – Which has the warmest feeling about it?
  – Which people would they most like to meet? etc.

● Ask the children to describe and comment upon:
  – the painting they most like in school
  – the picture they most admire at home
  – the best illustration in one of their story books
  – the best poster they see on their way to school
  – the most exciting of the current television commercials.

Works of art as storytelling

● Choose a work that is simple in its content, e.g. 'The Cholmondeley Sisters' (card 3), 'A Girl's Adventure' (4) or 'Autumn Leaves' (11). Ask the children to make a drawing of the picture in response to your describing it to them without them seeing it. When they have made their drawings, display and compare their versions with the original. Consider the different ways that they have made a drawing upon a similar theme to the artist.

● Give a small group of children a complex painting with a great deal of content, e.g. 'The Census at Bethlehem' (card 6), 'VE Day 1945' (9), 'Children's Swimming Pool' (2) or 'The Rout of San Romano' (21). Ask them to use viewfinders to select the six most important parts of the painting. Then ask them to make drawings of these and place them in sequence, like a 'story board', to explain what the painting is about.

Works of art as description

● Choose three or four paintings from this collection which describe in some detail one kind of person or place, e.g. the children in 'The Cholmondeley Sisters' (card 3), in 'The Census at Bethlehem' (6), in 'The Spinning Top' (14) or in 'Autumn Leaves' (11). Ask the children to discuss, write about and make drawings to explain how these artists have described children differently in their works.

● Look at the way that different artists have described weather in such paintings as 'Southwold' (card 16) and 'The Last of England' (15). Ask the children to make detailed colour studies to explain how an artist uses different methods to describe different weather conditions.

● Similarly, compare and describe the way that different artists draw and paint trees in such works as 'Tropical Storm with Tiger' (card 1), 'Twelve Squirrels in a Chennar Tree' (card 5), 'Landscape near Mont Majour' (13) and 'Mr and Mrs Andrews' (19).

Works of art as focus

Use work by artists to help children see the possibilities of making work upon a similar theme for themselves. There are many examples of this in the activities described to support the work in this pack. Here, you need to find ways to match the children's experience to that explored by the artist. For example:

– use a collection of house plants to recreate for the children the tropical jungle in Rousseau's 'Tropical Storm with Tiger' (card 1);
– use familiar beach furniture and accessories to construct part of the beach in Sir Stanley Spencer's 'Southwold' (16);
– use a selection of natural objects to put together landscapes upon a table top, similar to those used by Thomas Gainsborough (19);
– place before the children a goldfish bowl upon a check tablecloth, as in the painting by Henri Matisse (7).

This way of working in art is similar to that familiar strategy in the teaching of language where you use the work of other storytellers and poets to open up for children the possibilities of language. You can use similar methods to help children focus upon and see afresh familiar things within their own environment and to appreciate that there are different and equally effective ways to make images upon familiar themes. For example, in the activities related to the drawing of a harvest scene by Vincent Van Gogh (card 13), it is suggested that you compare this work with paintings of harvest scenes by other artists. This would be a useful way to introduce the children to making a painting in association with their own harvest festival.

Similarly, you could use Sir Stanley Spencer's 'Southwold' (16) in association with other paintings of people on beaches to help the children appreciate the different ways that they might make their own paintings about a visit to the seaside.

The activities that are described with each of the works of art in this pack will provide further clues about the rich variety of ways you can use paintings and sculptures with children. *Knowledge and Understanding in Art* describes in detail all the different methodologies you can use to help you deal with this aspect of the National Curriculum in Art.

THE WORK IN CONTEXT OF THE NATIONAL CURRICULUM

The Attainment Targets

Since all the work in this section begins with observing and talking about the work of other artists, craftworkers and designers, it is clearly rooted in Attainment Target 2: KNOWLEDGE AND UNDERSTANDING. In making their own and practical responses to these works, the children are addressing Attainment Target 1: INVESTIGATING AND MAKING. In responding to Millais' painting 'Autumn Leaves' (card 11), they are INVESTIGATING autumn leaves in their own environment and MAKING their own studies of leaves. Understanding of the artist's work will be extended through making practical responses and their knowledge of the work made more secure by building upon their observation and discussion through making.

The Programmes of Study

The practical activities suggested to acompany these works encompass the full range of the Programmes of Study for each of the two Attainment Targets. The Programmes of Study which are addressed in each of the activities are listed in the margins to the text for that activity. This will help you to keep a checklist of which Programmes of Study have been covered in the practical work generated through the study of each of the works of art and design in this collection.

The general requirements, Attainment Targets and Programmes of Study provided in the National Curriculum guidelines for Art at Key Stages 1 and 2 are reproduced below and on pages 16 to 19.

General requirements

1   In all key stages pupils should be given opportunities to:
- undertake a balanced programme of art, craft and design activities which clearly builds on previous work and takes account of previous achievement;
- work individually, in groups, and as a whole class;
- make appropriate use of information technology;

- work in two and three dimensions and on a variety of scales;
- evaluate their own and others' work.

2   Pupils should understand and appreciate art in a variety of genres and styles from a variety of cultures, Western and non-Western.

3   'Art' should be interpreted to mean 'art, craft and design' throughout and 'artists' should be interpreted to mean 'artists, craftworkers and designers'.

ACROSS THE CURRICULUM

Although all the work that may be generated through the use of these resources lies clearly within the National Curriculum for Art, much of the work will have implications for and relevance to other National Curriculum subjects. In undertaking this work the children will also be addressing the Attainment Targets and Programmes of Study for other subjects. You will begin to recognise these opportunities for cross-curricular reference as you work your way through the text.

English

In all this work there are many opportunities for the rich use of oral and written language as children are encouraged to share their perceptions of these works of art with you and with each other.

History

There is a particularly strong link between AT2 in Art – KNOWLEDGE AND UNDERSTANDING – and AT3 in History – THE USE OF HISTORICAL EVIDENCE. Many of the works included in this collection are important historical documents and tell us much about the way that people lived in past times, how they lived, what they wore, what they made and used and how their lives were different to ours today.

Science

In many of the paintings included in this collection, there are observations and activities suggested that relate to the Programmes of Study in Science that are concerned with the study of colour and light.

Technology

Some of the activities recommended in this pack will lend themselves naturally to extensions into designing and making artefacts within the context of Technology. Some of the works contain images of artefacts in previous use, which can be interestingly contrasted with their present-day equivalents. The social context of many of the works will suggest interesting design problems that the children might address: e.g. 'How might you trap the tiger in Rousseau's jungle?'

Music

Two of the works – 'Green and Blue Music' (card 23) and 'Broadway Boogie-Woogie' (card 24) – make specific references to musical activities; others present opportunities for finding or composing musical equivalents for the images presented.

Religious education

Because so many of these works were made within the context of different times and different cultures there are rich possibilities for using them to extend the children's understanding of the way that artists have made works of art to celebrate the beliefs of the communities they served.

Cross-curricular examples

The three project descriptions which follow illustrate the way that a group of works of art from this collection may be used as a major resource within a cross-curricular theme. They describe the activities that might be undertaken in Key Stages 1 and 2 within the following topics:

● Protection
● Colour and light
● Families

They should help you to see that in any cross-curricular topic you undertake, there are real opportunities for using works of art to extend children's experience and enquiry within the theme.

TOPIC: PROTECTION

Using the following works:

6 The Census at Bethlehem	**16** Southwold
12 Mr and Mrs Clark and Percy	**18** Goggle Head
15 The Last of England	**21** The Rout of San Romano

Investigate and focus

● How many kinds of protection can you find in these works? Remember it is not only people who need protecting but things as well.

● All clothing protects us in some way. What other things do we need protecting from apart from the sun, wind and rain? Make a list of these things.

● Find and make drawings of things in these works that protect people from the cold, rain and heat and from each other.

Key Stage 1 Activities

● Make studies from these works to show the differences between clothes that are worn in cold weather and those worn in hot weather or indoors. Has central heating made a difference to things we wear in the winter today compared with many years ago?

● How many different kinds of things do we put on our feet to protect them? Make a list of as many as you can find in these paintings and make drawings of two very different kinds of footwear.

● What sort of 'protection' do we have that we don't wear? Begin with umbrellas (in 'The Last of England') – how many more can you find? Think about transport and buildings and the way they protect us.

● Find examples of things that protect you in school. Find examples of things that protect you at home.

Key Stage 2 Activities

● People not only protect themselves from the elements but also from damage by wearing protective clothing. Sunglasses protect the eyes from harmful rays, helmets are worn on building sites and lifejackets at sea. How many different kinds of protective clothing can you find? Make studies of different kinds of protective headgear. Design a protective garment to protect you from something you consider dangerous.

● In 'The Last of England', cabbages are stored in netting around the boat to keep them fresh for a long voyage. How do we protect food and keep it fresh today? How do you store food at home, when you bring it to school, when you go on a journey and take a picnic?

● Armour has been made over the centuries to protect soldiers in battle. Compare the armour worn in 'The Battle of San Romano' with that worn by soldiers today to protect them from bullets and bombs.

● The sea wall and groynes in 'Southwold' protect the town and the beach from the sea. Can you find other ways of protecting the environment in your own area?

TOPIC: COLOUR AND LIGHT

Using the following works:

Investigate and focus

● Where does light come from? How many sources of light do we see and use in our everyday lives?

● How does light change things? Why does it pass through some things and not through others?

● Why does colour change in different kinds of light?

● What makes shadows and reflections?

Key Stage 1 Activities

● Make a collection of leaves and by holding them against the light and in different parts of the room. See how they change colour and which ones let most light through them.

● Make a colour chart of the leaves collected and compare these with those in the painting 'Autumn Leaves'.

● Make careful colour studies of all the different shades of colour in one leaf. Place a few leaves on a window sill and over a period of time note and record how their colour changes with exposure to light.

● Make collections of pebbles and compare their colours with those on the beach at 'Southwold'. Make colour studies of the pebbles and compare these with the colours when the pebbles are placed in a tray of water.

● Find the lightest and darkest parts of the classroom. Observe the way that familiar objects change colour in different parts of the room and compare these changes with the appearance of objects in the paintings of interiors.

● Make maps of shadows in the playground by outlining them with chalk at different times of the day. Make paintings and drawings of 'Me and my Shadow'.

Key Stage 2 Activities

● Observe and make careful studies of the way that the colours and shadows of familiar natural and made objects change as their positions are changed in relation to the light or when they are lit from different directions by artificial light sources.

● Compare the appearance of their own faces when viewed in different kinds of surfaces – in a mirror, reflected in a spoon or in a window.

● Observe and compare the reflections in water in the paintings 'Goldfish' and 'Children's Swimming Pool'. Place simple objects (e.g. a spoon or twig) in glasses of water and observe and record the distortions in their appearance.

● Observe the way that moving water distorts the appearance of things within it – in a local stream, in the swimming pool or in water trays in the classroom.

● Collect photographs of landscapes taken at different times of the day and in different weather conditions. Talk and write about these. Using natural objects and toys, construct small landscapes with figures in shoe or similar boxes. Use light sources and colour filters to change their appearance and make paintings of their landscapes in different 'moods' of light and colour.

TOPIC: OUR FAMILIES

Use the following works:	**3** The Cholmondeley Sisters	**15** The Last of England
	6 The Census at Bethlehem	**16** Southwold
	11 Autumn Leaves	**19** Mr and Mrs Andrews
	12 Mr and Mrs Clark and Percy	

Focus and investigation

● What is a family and who belongs within it – relations, friends and neighbours? What kind of families can we find in these works?

● How do families live and play together? What do they do at different times of the year?

● How has family life changed over the years? How is family life different in different times and cultures?

Key Stage 1 Activities

● Collect photographs of their own families – identify and write about their own family network.

● Make drawings to identify their place within the family, special friendships, likenesses and differences etc.

● Family occasions: collect photographs and pictures of special events within the family – birthdays, christenings, holidays, festivals etc.

Compare these with the events taking place in 'The Cholmondeley Sisters', 'The Census at Bethlehem', 'Southwold' and 'Autumn Leaves'. Make up stories about what is happening in these paintings and then write about and make their own paintings of their families engaged in similar activities.

● Read stories about family life in other times and cultures and compare these with their own.

Key Stage 2 Activities

● Collect photographs of themselves at different ages and memorabilia that remind them of when they were younger. Use the pictures and the objects as source material to make a 'timeline' series of drawings about their own history within the family.

● Collect stories and accounts from parents, grandparents and other family friends about their family childhood – make comparisons and write about the differences.

● Use the paintings to surmise about family life in the different times represented in them. How are they different to family life today?

● Use 'Mr and Mrs Andrews' and 'Mr and Mrs Clark and Percy' to generate discussion about how people within the family present themselves for a special occasion. Compare these portraits with wedding photographs, and photographs of themselves and friends and family dressed for a party, a disco, a holiday etc. Use these as source materials for painting and storytelling.

● Make maps and diagrams to show where different members live, within the community or across the country or in places abroad. Use 'The Last of England' to generate discussion about why families are often scattered about a country, why people have to leave home to work and study. How do families keep in touch with each other? Write about reunions and visits to other family members who live far away.

SUPPORTING INFORMATION

This is provided for each of the works of art in this collection and should help you to use them effectively and to consider ways in which you might extend the activities beyond those suggested here.

Resources: what you need to collect and make available to support this work.

Materials: what you need beyond those normally available for work in Art.

Topics: some of the general and cross-curricular themes this work might relate to.

Other works by the artist: other works that you might use with the children.

Comparisons: work by other artists which makes for interesting comparison with this work.

Bibliography: some of the publications currently available about the artist's work.

EXTENDING THE COLLECTION

We hope that this collection of works of art will encourage you to collect and find further works to extend the range of reference material you can offer to children in your school. You might begin by seeking out other work by the same artist in books, posters, postcards and magazine articles or you might look for work on similar themes made by other artists. Making comparisons between paintings on similar themes by different artists can be a very rewarding way to encourage children to investigate paintings and can stimulate 'collecting' pictures as a class activity. In *Knowledge and Understanding in Art* you will find useful and practical advice as to how you can put together a good school collection of reference and resource material about the work of artists, craft-workers and designers.

The General Bibliography will offer you some starting points for seeking more information about the work of the artists featured in this collection and their contemporaries.

Key Stage 1

Attainment Target 1: *INVESTIGATING AND MAKING*

The development of visual perception and the skills associated with investigating and making in art, craft and design.

End of Key Stage statement	*Programme of Study*
By the end of Key Stage 1, pupils should be able to:	Pupils should:
A represent in visual form what they observe, remember and imagine.	i record observations from direct experience of the natural and made environments.
	ii respond to memory and the imagination.
B select from a range of items they have collected and use them as a basis for their work.	iii collect and sort images, objects and source material.
C work practically and imaginatively with a variety of materials and methods exploring the elements of art.	iv explore a range of materials, tools and techniques.
	v explore how images can be made through using line and tone, working with a variety of tools and materials.
	vi explore colour-mixing from primary colours.
	vii explore and recreate pattern and texture in natural and made forms.
	viii explore the use of shape form and space in making images and artefacts.
	ix make three-dimensional work for a variety of purposes.
D implement simple changes in their work in the light of progress made.	x review their work and modify it as they see the need for change.
	xi talk about their work and how they have made it.

Attainment Target 2: *KNOWLEDGE AND UNDERSTANDING*

The development of visual literacy and knowledge and understanding of art, craft and design including the history of art, our diverse artistic heritage and a variety of other artistic traditions, together with the ability to make practical connections between this and pupil's own work.

End of Key Stage stagement

By the end of Key Stage 1, pupils should be able to:

A recognise different kinds of art.

B identify some of the ways in which art has changed, distinguishing between work in the past and present.

C begin to make connections between their own work and that of other artists.

Programme of Study

Pupils should:

i identify examples of art in school and the environment.

ii identify different kinds of art, present and past.

iii look at and talk about examples of work of well-known artists from a variety of periods and cultures.

iv represent in their own work their understanding of the theme or mood of a work of art.

Key Stage 2

Attainment Target 1: *INVESTIGATING AND MAKING*

The development of visual perception and the skills associated with investigating and making in art, craft and design.

End of Key Stage statement	Programme of Study
By the end of Key Stage 2, pupils should be able to:	Pupils should:
A communicate ideas and feelings in visual form based on what they observe, remember and imagine	i select and record images and ideas from first-hand observation
	ii respond to memory and imagination using a range of media
	iii use a sketchbook to record observations and ideas.
B develop an idea or theme for their work, drawing on visual and other sources and discuss their methods.	iv experiment with ideas suggested by different source materials and explain how they have used them to develop their work.
C experiment with and apply their knowledge of the elements of art, choosing appropriate media.	v apply their knowledge and experience of different materials, tools and techniques, using them experimentally and expressively.
	vi experiment with different qualities of line and tone in making images.
	vii apply the principles of colour mixing in making various kinds of images.
	viii experiment with pattern and texture in designing and making images and artefacts.
	ix experiment with ways of representing shape, form and space.
	x plan and make three-dimensional structures using various materials and for a variety of purposes.
D modify their work in the light of its development and their original intentions.	xi adapt or modify their work in order to realise their ideas and explain and justify the changes they have made.
	xii use a developing specialist vocabulary to describe their work and what it means.

Attainment Target 2: *KNOWLEDGE AND UNDERSTANDING*

The development of visual literacy and knowledge and understanding of art, craft and design including the history of art, our diverse artistic heritage and a variety of other artistic traditions, together with the ability to make practical connections between this and pupils' own work.

End of Key Stage statement	*Programme of Study*
By the end of Key Stage 2, pupils should be able to:	Pupils should:
A identify different kinds of art and their purposes.	i compare the different purposes of familiar visual forms and discuss their findings with their teachers and peers. ii understand and use subject-specific terms such as landscape, still-life, mural.
B begin to identify the characteristics of art in a variety of genres from different periods, cultures and traditions, showing some knowledge of the related historical background.	iii look at and discuss art from early, Renaissance and later periods in order to start to understand the way in which art has developed and the contribution of influential artists or groups of artists to that development. iv identify and compare some of the methods and materials that artists use.
C make imaginative use in their own work of a developing knowledge of the work of other artists.	v experiment with some of the methods and approaches used by other artists, and use these imaginatively to inform their own work.

1 'Tropical Storm with Tiger', 1891
Henri Rousseau (1844–1910)

(130 cm × 162 cm)

National Gallery, London

ABOUT THE ARTIST

Henri Rousseau was the son of a shopkeeper. His mother's family had been distinguished in the French army and at the age of 19 Henri joined the 52nd Infantry Regimental Band where he played the saxophone. When he left the army Henri became a customs officer in Paris where, at each of the city gates, merchants were charged a tax on their goods. He began to paint when he was about 40 years old. At first, people didn't understand his work but he was convinced of their worth and believed that the public would come to enjoy them one day.

Henri Rousseau continued to paint for the rest of his life. His friends helped and supported him. His work began to be taken more seriously towards the end of his life. He is thought to have made about 140 paintings and 200 drawings: some of which were destroyed; others were lost.

Rousseau concentrated mainly on subjects which reflected his great interests in life: his family and friends, the army and sporting pictures, landscapes, jungles and storytelling scenes.

ABOUT THE WORK

Other **primitive painters** have their own view of life. Like Rousseau, they have no formal education in art but have become expert in the use of different media because of their passionate belief in the value of the art they make. Look at the work of Beryl Cook and Grandma Moses.

Other painters who have worked on similar subjects include Stubbs and Bewick. Many Indian miniatures have tigers in them. You could also read William Blake's poem 'Tiger, tiger, burning bright' and/or an extract from Rudyard Kipling's *The Mowgli Stories* to the children to extend their understanding and to develop their language skills.

DISCUSSION POINTS

● This picture is one of a set that Rousseau painted later in his life. He called them his 'Mexican' pictures; but although he was in the army there is no record of him ever having been to Mexico. However, in his later years, he did visit the zoo and tropical plant house in Paris frequently. Could he have used the animals and plants as reference material for his pictures? Look carefully at the plants in the picture. Are there any you recognise?

- Rousseau told his friends he was using 22 different greens in one of his jungle paintings. How many can you see here? What other colours has he used?

- Rousseau also told his friends that when he was painting these pictures of jungles and wild animals they sometimes made him feel frightened. Are there any pictures that you find frightening?

- Have you ever been to a zoo or a circus? What do you think about animals being shut in? Do you think they would be happier in the wild?

- Which countries do tigers come from and what sort of jungle do they actually live in? (India, Nepal, Bangladesh and Asia – not tropical rain forest.) Find some pictures or photographs of the areas of the world in which tigers live.

- Can you find any poems or stories about tigers (e.g. William Blake's 'Tiger, tiger, burning bright'; Rudyard Kipling's 'The Mowgli Stories')? Many Indian poems and stories mention tigers.

- Looking at pictures and photographs of things does not tell us what they are really like. If you want to know more about how tigers move and behave, you could look at one of their relations – the domestic cat.

ACTIVITIES

- Encourage the children to choose a few house plants, either from around the school or from home. Look at the pattern of the leaves and flowers, if there are any. Try to find some with similar shapes to the ones in the 'Tropical Storm with Tiger' picture. Talk about the variety of greens. Are they dark, light, blue or yellowish? Are they all the same, or similar? How do they look when you see them one behind the other?

Key Stage I
I(i), I(iii), I(vi), I(vii)

- Using wax crayons or oil pastels and buff/grey sugar paper, make drawings of the structure of one of the plants.

- Talk with the children about what it might feel like to be in a jungle. Ask them to imagine they are 5 centimetres high. How would the

Key Stage I
I(ii)

plants look to them then? They could make a picture of themselves in the jungle using the plants they have seen. They could create their own collage. They don't need to paint all of themself in their picture, but we should be able to see a bit of them if we look hard.

Key Stage I

I(iii), I(ix), General requirements

● Using your knowledge of mathematics, make a net to show the children how to make a small box. It should be an open-fronted cube, about 8–10 centimetres across. Look at Rousseau's painting and try to see it in layers of foreground, middle and background, with all the plants growing up trees at the sides and branches hanging down from the top. Draw, cut out and paint each layer and stick it into the box (they will need tabs on each section for this). They will then have made their own three-dimensional version of the painting. Don't forget to put in the tiger! The children can add other animals if they like.

EVALUATION

● Have the children developed a greater awareness of plant structures and colours?

● Were they able to distinguish more and more tones and shades of each colour as they looked at the painting and at the real plants?

SUPPORTING INFORMATION

Resources:
— photographs of jungles
— selection of house plants
— photographs of tigers and other wild animals
— stories and poems about tigers e.g. 'Tiger, tiger, burning bright' by William Blake

Materials:
mathematical net for open cube – 8 cm × 10 cm across

Topics:
camouflage; habitats

Other works by the artist:
'Virgin Forest' (Kunstmuseum, Basle, Switzerland)
'Tiger Hunt' (Columbus Gallery, Ohio, USA)
'Bouquet of Flowers' (Tate Gallery, London)
'Surprise' (National Gallery, London)
'Sleeping Gypsy' (Museum of Modern Art, New York)

Comparisons:

'Cheetah with two Indian Attendants' by George Stubbs (Manchester City Art Gallery)

'Akbar Hunting with Cheetahs near Agra' by Dharm Das (Victoria & Albert Museum, London)

'Tippoo's Tiger' from South India (Victoria & Albert Museum)

Bibliography:

Vallier, D, *Henri Rousseau* (Bonfini Press)

Pantelic, B, *Primitive Art* (Bracken Books)

Shattuck, Behar, Hoog and Rubin, *Henri Rousseau* (Museum of Modern Art, New York)

2 'Children's Swimming Pool, 11 o'clock Saturday morning, August 1969' Leon Kossof (1926–)

(152.4 cm × 205.7 cm)

Saatchi Collection, London

ABOUT THE ARTIST

Leon Kossof was born of Russian-Jewish parents who came to settle in London's East End. He began drawing when he was 12 years old. After his schooling, he went to St Martin's School of Art (1949–52). In the evenings he studied with a man who had a strong influence at the time, David Bomberg. Then Leon went to the Royal College, from 1953 to 1956. His first one-man show was held at the Beaux Arts Gallery in London in 1957. He has lived and painted in London all his life and has concentrated on painting his family, especially his father, and scenes of the city. His most usual subjects are city streets, bomb sites, building sites, excavations and railways, and several paintings of swimming pools.

ABOUT THIS WORK

This is one of the paintings that Leon Kossof based on memories of his childhood and it is a picture of the children's swimming pool in Willesden. He has used a restricted range of colours to create this particular atmosphere – a subtle range of blues and greens for the special effect produced by water and glass. He has also created a very busy scene by crowding the figures together. The paint he has used is very thick, so he has been able to draw and paint at the same time. He has chosen to show us lots of children as they might be when you remember something, not as you might really see them.

DISCUSSION POINTS

● Perhaps the most compelling starting point is the wealth of activity in this picture. There are children swimming, floating, diving and queueing up to dive. Others are at the side watching and some are sitting on the edge of the pool. When you go to a swimming pool is it usually as busy as this? Or has the artist tried to put into his picture all the things that can happen and show them all at once? Do you ever do this with your pictures?

- How many pools are there? This might seem a simple question but the painting is so full of activity it is easy to miss the second pool in the background. Look carefully at the shapes of the pools. They are shown as going away from us, so they are not square; they get smaller the further away they are. Can you find any other shapes around which get smaller in this way – like the netball court or the football pitch? How might you draw these things to show how they *look*?

- The atmosphere in this picture is created as much by the colour as by things within it. Look hard. Can you smell the pool and hear the noise? Although there are reds and blues and yellows, they all seem to be part of the whole, seen through the special light you often get at a swimming pool. How has this been created?

- Try to find some reproductions of the swimming pool paintings by the Yorkshire artist David Hockney. They are very different. Comparing the two styles may help to focus in on the special qualities that both have. Look particularly at the way that paint and colour have been used and see if the shapes of the pools are similar.

ACTIVITIES

- Ask the children to look carefully at the range of blues and greens in the picture. Using powder colour, ready mix or oil pastels, make the colours you can see. Begin with the range of blues, then the greens and only then move on to the other colours. Look at what they have produced. There should be three sets of colours which they could use to make their own swimming pool picture. Go on to do this if the children are very familiar with swimming pools and you feel they will enjoy it.

Key Stage I
I(iii), I(iv), I(vi)

- The texture of the paint in this picture is very thick and fluid. It could almost have been put on with a palette knife. You could try an experiment here to match the appearance of this paint. Use powder colour mixed with a little water and add some PVA glue to it. This will make the paint very thick and also rather shiny. Try putting it on to the paper with a large brush. When the children have had time to practise with this and find out what it will do, ask them to use it to make a painting. They could do their own idea of a swimming pool or they could use another suitable subject to match these colours, like a landscape or a conservatory.

Key Stage I
I(iii), I (iv), I(x)

- If you have a swimming pool near you, take the children there to do some drawing. Ask them to make quick sketches of some of the swimmers and how they look half in and half out of the water, and to make separate sketches of the water. These drawings are best

Key Stage I
I(i), I(iv), I(v)

made quickly and directly with wax crayons or oil pastels. They could then look at the painting again and do their own interpretation of one of the groups of figures.

EVALUATION

● How much did the children learn about mixing colour and adding glue to make it thicker?

● Did they enjoy using the thicker texture of paint?

● Could they think of other times when it might be useful to be able to use thicker paint?

● Were the children able to feel the noise and excitement in this picture of the swimming pool?

● Were they able to appreciate that Leon Kossoff painted it from memory?

● It would be worth a little time to discuss what memories the children think they might have when they are much older. What memories do they think might last?

SUPPORTING INFORMATION

Resource:
— visit to local swimming pool

Materials:
powder colour mixed with PVA

Topics:
leisure; water

Other works by the artist:
'Family Party' (Saatchi Collection, London)
'School Building, Willesden' (Saatchi Collection, London)
'A Street in Willesden' (Saatchi Collection, London)

Comparisons:
'A Bigger Splash' by David Hockney (Tate Gallery, London)
'Bathing at Asniers' by Georges Seurat (National Gallery, London)
'July, The Seaside' by L S Lowry (Arts Council Collection)

Bibliography:
Lucie Smith, E, Cohen, J and Higgins, J, The New British Painting (Phaidon)
Hicks, A, New British Art in the Saatchi Collection (Thames & Hudson)
Elliot, D, Leon Kossoff, Paintings from a decade (Museum of Modern Art, Oxford)

3 'The Cholmondeley Sisters', circa 1600–1610 British School

(88.9 cm × 172.7 cm)

Tate Gallery, London

ABOUT THE ARTIST

The artist who painted this picture didn't sign it and the name has been forgotten. Lots of pictures, poems, music and writing are anonymous, but this does not spoil our enjoyment of them nor does it mean we think they are any less important. Indeed, sometimes where work has been done in a particular style, whether painted or written, it has been falsely attributed to another person. For example, quite a lot of scholars have argued for and against William Shakespeare having written all that is credited to him. It is interesting to ask how much a name can affect our judgement. If we value something is it because we feel it is really worthwhile or because some currently popular person did it? You could use pop music as an example.

ABOUT THIS WORK

Style comes into this piece of work in another way. It isn't just the style of the individual but also the style or the way that people in one particular group painted in one place and time. Other paintings of people done at this time were treated in the same way. King Henry VIII and Queen Elizabeth I had many portraits painted: the same methods of painting were used; that is, with the person looking straight at us and with lots of minute detail in their clothes and jewellery. You can tell what things the people of the time thought were important. Clearly, elaborate clothes with lots of embroidery, jewels and decoration were essential to your rank and importance. England was becoming a great world power under Elizabeth I and riches were flowing in as a result of voyages of discovery. In turn, people could afford to have paintings made of how they looked and of certain events in their lives. There are many pictures of processions through London with Queen Elizabeth I at their centre. Try to find the painting 'Royal Procession' by Dennis Alsoot, or one of the other procession paintings, to learn more about this period in history.

DISCUSSION POINTS

- This type of picture is called a 'double portrait' because it is intended to be a likeness of two ladies. Are there any twins in school? Are they 'identical' or different? Do twins run in families? Are there any two people in the class with the same birthday?

- Do the babies in the picture look like real children? Do you know why they were painted like this?

- Can you find any differences between the two ladies? Look at their faces first. Then look carefully at the colour and shape of their eyes and those of the babies.

- Look at the patterns round the edge of their ruffs. Are they the same or different? What do the shapes remind you of? Look at a banknote and you will see that we still use patterns in our pictures of important people. Sterling banknotes have a picture of the Queen on them. She is shown wearing a crown or tiara. Are the patterns similar to those in the painting?

- There may be an historic house or National Trust property nearby which dates back to the 1600s. A visit there could stimulate interest and understanding of the period and make links with local historical events.

ACTIVITIES

- Talk about portraits that are made today – they range from the informal holiday snapshots to christening and wedding photographs and school photographs taken by professional photographers. Today, very few people have their portraits painted by artists as these pictures tend to be very expensive.

Key Stage I
I(i), I(iv), I(v), I(x)

- The children could pair portraits of each other so that they have a record of how they look now. It would be best to draw/paint it lifesize so that there is room in the picture to put in all the details. Remind them to look carefully at the colours and shape of the eyes, at the colours of the skin and hair, and to notice how they are not all one colour but change with the light and shade. The children might try using a black background like the one in the picture.

Key Stage I
I(iii), I(vii), I(ix)

- Using cardboard, paper and paint, the children could design and make their own crowns or headdresses for a party.

I(i), I(vii)

- The children could make a painting, on black paper, of the lady they like best in the picture. They will have to look carefully because the ladies appear so alike at a first glance. They should take time to study as closely as they can exactly how the clothes and faces are painted so that they can get it right. Then you will know which of the two ladies they chose without having to ask.

EVALUATION

- Have the children appreciated why portraits are made and all the different forms they can take?

- Were they able to compare and evaluate for themselves the stages of importance in the order of portraits from family snaps to banknotes and oil paintings?

- Did the children begin to develop a sense of the very different times the Tudor sisters in the painting lived in?

SUPPORTING INFORMATION

Resources:
- banknotes
- holiday and family photographs
- photographs of twins/sisters

Topics:
the Tudors; families and relationships; dress

Other works:
'Portrait of Queen Elizabeth I' by an unknown artist (National Portrait Gallery, London)
'Queen Elizabeth First' by Nicholas Hilliard (National Portrait Gallery)
'Queen Elizabeth I' by Marcus Gheerats (Woburn Abbey, Bedfordshire)

Comparisons:
'The Painter's Daughters' by Thomas Gainsborough (National Gallery, London)
'The Graham Children' by William Hogarth (Tate Gallery, London)
'Rose et Bleu' by August Renoir (Museum of Art, San Paulo)

4 'A Girl's Adventure', 1922 Paul Klee (1879–1940)

(Water colour, 44 cm × 32 cm)

Tate Gallery, London

ABOUT THE ARTIST

Paul Klee was born in Switzerland, the son of a German music teacher and a Swiss mother. In his childhood, he was equally interested and competent in art and music. He could have chosen a career in either. However, he decided to train as an artist and went to Munich to study. He settled in Germany and married a pianist. In his early days, he drew constantly and studied nature; his landscape drawings were very realistic. Then Paul Klee began to travel to expand his horizons. In 1908 he discovered the work of Van Gogh and Matisse, and for a time he joined '**The Blaue Reiter**' (Blue Rider) group of artists. They believed in individual expression and a new way of using colour, not merely to imitate nature but to add to and enhance it. Klee also got to know about current developments, including the **Cubists** (one of whom, Picasso, is also featured in this pack – card 10).

Paul Klee also travelled to Italy and to the ruins of Carthage (Tunisia), and in 1928 he went to Egypt. The things he saw on these travels influenced his work. He was fascinated by Arabic script and **hieroglyphics** and these appear in some of his work. Up to the age of 35 he only painted in watercolour – as in our example. He knew groups of painters who believed in similar ways of painting, although he was always an individualist. Paul Klee believed in searching beyond the appearance of things to reveal that which was not obvious to the eye – the feelings and fantasies that we weave around the things we see in the real world. He called his work 'picture poems' and said he was trying to reach the heart of creation. Around 1925, when he had been teaching for some time, he wrote about his experiences in a book called *Pedagogical Sketchbook*. The most famous quote from his writing is: 'Art does not reproduce what we see, it makes us see.'

In 1935 he escaped from Germany to Switzerland when Hitler began his persecution of artists. He worked in Switzerland until his death. He left over 9000 pieces of work, plus his diaries and other writings.

ABOUT THIS WORK

This picture was painted when Paul Klee was 53 and well into his own imaginative style. He is showing us his idea of a young girl having an adventure, but he leaves a lot to our imaginations too. A first look at this painting shows us a girl – we expect that because of the title – then we begin to look around the figure and discover all sorts of creatures; then back to the girl to find that parts of her are also part of the background. Klee uses his ability to weave patterns to take us into the picture and into a magic world.

DISCUSSION POINTS

● Beginning with the central figure, we know from the title she is a girl; however, she is certainly more like a dream girl than a real one. What do you think of when we mention 'young', as opposed to 'old'? Small noses and pink lips are characteristics of the very young. Now write a list of other features you associate with babies and young children. Think about the changes that happen as we grow up. What differences are there between you and pupils in a secondary school and grown-ups?

● How many animals can you find in the picture? The longer you look at this painting, the more you will be able to see in it. Have you spotted the second figure?

● Although things are recognisable, they are more dream-like than real. Do you ever dream about things? Do you remember your dreams and would you like to describe them?

● What makes people or animals look friendly or dangerous? What makes them look kind or cruel? Do you think the creatures in the picture are friendly? How much depends on eyes and expressions?

● Paul Klee has used colour and line to make his picture. The girl's head and body are light and shown against a dark background which makes them stand out. Most of the other things are part of the background, even the red arrow which links with the other spots of red. Do these things stand out as much as the pinks and yellows? Look at other pictures and around the room to see which colours stand out against different backgrounds.

ACTIVITIES

● If you were able to find colours that stood out one against another, you could ask the children to 'take a line for a walk'. Then use water-colours or crayons to fill in the shapes and explore using one colour against another. This is purely a colour exercise. Use A5 cartridge

Key Stage I
I(v), I(vi)

paper and have a spare piece to practise the colours. Use a biro to draw the line but don't make it too long or the areas will get very small. Fill each section with colour. The accent here is on care, precision and accuracy, taking pride in being able to keep exactly to the lines; so if using watercolours the children will need good quality, fine brushes. Ask the children to choose colours which contrast with each other so that one stands out against another.

Key Stage 1

1(ii), 1(iii), 1(viii)

● Using coloured crayons and white paper, ask the children to imagine and draw themselves in a 'dream world' or to draw something they might like to dream about. They should use the crayons first to colour in the areas and add the dark line later – dark brown, blue or purple, not black. They can map it out in light pencil first if they want to.

Key Stage 1

1(iii), 1(vii),
1(ix), 1(x)

● Focus on the creatures in the picture. Each one is made up of sections – circles, cones and triangles. Ask the children to draw some of these birds and animals and some more of their own using similar shapes. Cut them out and use them as templates to cut out coloured papers or fabrics. If you are making a paper collage, it could be A2 or A3; if it is a fabric collage, make it at least A2 card and stick the fabric down firmly, as it needs to be fairly flat to be effective.

EVALUATION

● In your discussion at the end of one of the activities it would be worth pinning up the children's work alongside the Klee painting to give them an opportunity to see if their colours stand out against each other as his do. They could do their own evaluation and talk about how successful they felt they had been, and explain why.

● Did the children understand that Paul Klee could draw very well but chose to work in this more decorative way?

● Were the children excited by talking about the creatures in this picture?

● Were they able to appreciate a sense of humour and fun in the painting?

SUPPORTING INFORMATION

Resources:
– photographs of children

Topics:
fiction; stories about dreams and strange adventures

Other works by the artist:
'Seaside Town in the South of France' (Tate Gallery, London)
'Fish Magic' (Philadelphia Museum of Arts, USA)
'A Child's Game' (Felix Klee Collection, Berne, West Germany)

Comparisons:
'Femmes, Oiseau au Claire de Lune' by Joan Miro (Tate Gallery, London)
'I, the Village' by Marc Chagall (Museum of Modern Art, New York)
'Girl with a Dove' by Pablo Picasso

Bibliography:
Raboff, E, *Klee* (Ernest Benn)
Partsch, S, *Paul Klee* (Taschen)

5 'Twelve Squirrels in a Chennar Tree', circa 1630 Abu'l Hasan (1589–1650)

India Office Library, London.

ABOUT THE ARTIST

The Mughal Empire was founded early in the 16th century by a man called Babur, one of whose ancestors was Genghis Khan. He inherited much and won more through battles, building up an enormous empire. He was a highly educated man and with his great wealth he enhanced the rich traditions of art and writing. He also built a great many fine buildings, employing over one thousand masons. Gold, silver and jewels were made into fine jewellery. The British Crown Jewels have a diamond from this collection called the 'Koh-i-Noor'.

When Babur died in 1530, a power struggle followed until his great grandson became emperor in 1605, taking the title Jahangir ('World seizer'). Along with the vast country, he inherited incredible wealth. He also employed a large number of the finest artists and craftsmen. One of these was Aqa Reza, an Iranian artist whose son Abu'l Hasan grew up here and was trained by his father from an early age. Abu'l Hasan became one of the most famous artists and was given the title Nadiru'l Zaman, which means 'wonder of the age'.

ABOUT THIS WORK

The artist has chosen to compose the picture so that everything is visible; nothing is hidden behind something else. Apart from the man and the tree, there are 12 squirrels and about 35 birds in the picture!

THINGS TO DO

● The area of the world known as the Mughal Empire was enormous in the 16th century and covered most of the area of present-day India, from the Himalayas to Bombay in the south. From east to west it included all that is now known as Bangladesh and Pakistan. Find an atlas and see how big this area was in relation to Great Britain. Abu'l Hasan spent a lot of his early life living in Allahabad.

● Jahangir travelled a lot and took Abu'l Hassan and many of his fellow artists with him to record the people, fruit and flowers of each region they visited. As the Mughal Empire covered such a vast area they saw many unusual and unfamiliar things. Studies they made of the flowers were then made into patterns to decorate the borders of manuscripts and paintings. Find a book of Indian writing and let the children look for the way the artist has decorated the pages.

● An amazingly rich variety of decorative arts flourished at this time. Find pictures or examples of Indian carpets, fabrics and embroidery. Ask the children to look at the intricate detail and the harmony of the colours.

● The Mughal Emperors were well known for their splendid architecture, some of which survives to this day. The most famous of the buildings was built by Jahangir's son, Shah Jahan, in memory of his wife who died in 1631. The 'Taj Mahal' is one of the great wonders of the world. Find a picture of it.

ACTIVITIES

● Give the children small viewfinders (pieces of black card measuring about 4 cm X 6 cm with a rectangular hole cut in the centre). Ask them to isolate any group of birds. Using watercolours or coloured pencils, draw or paint what they see. They should make their drawings much larger than those in the picture to allow room to put in the detail. Remember, Abu'l Hasan was a great artist so he was able to paint very fine detail with great control.

Key Stage I
General requirements, I(i)

● The children could look carefully at the squirrels. Talk with them about how no two squirrels are in the same position: some are going up the tree, others are coming down; while the babies who are at the centre of the picture have only their heads showing.

Key Stage I
I(i), I(v)

● What other creatures do we see making so many different movements? Ask the children to look out of the window and make quick drawings of the birds as they fly and walk about. Or they could do drawings of pets at home or of a pet in the classroom.

● In the 'Twelve Squirrels in a Chennar Tree' painting the background must have been painted first because there is so much detail in the foreground. When the children paint pictures of their own they should think about the order in which they should do things. If you have a good view outside your classroom window, ask the children to try making a painting of this, beginning with the background and working their way forward.

Key Stage I
I(i), I(v), I(viii)

Key Stage I
General require-
ments. I(vii), I(ix)

Key Stage I
I(i), I(iii)

● The most brilliantly coloured parts of this picture are the leaves. Study the shapes carefully, or look at any leaves you have growing near your school. Ask the children to make a cardboard block and print on paper or fabric using the wide variety of colours they can see in the picture.

EVALUATION

● Did the children learn more about Indian art and were they able to appreciate and begin to understand a society that valued the arts so highly?

● Did they enjoy counting the birds and animals and making their own bird and animal pictures?

● Were the children able to understand the remarkable composition and arrangement of the painting which shows all the things of interest and avoids overlapping any of the objects of interest?

● Were they able to understand how complex patterns can be built up from simple printing blocks by overprinting in different colours?

SUPPORTING INFORMATION

Resources:
- map of India, Pakistan and Bangladesh
- collection of leaves
- photographs of birds, squirrels and pets
- photograph of the Taj Mahal, Agra, India

Materials:
viewfinders; materials for making paper/card printing blocks

Topics:
India/ The Near East

Other works:
'Akbar Hunting' – Mughal (Victoria & Albert Museum, London)
'Zebra' – Mughal (Victoria & Albert Museum)

Comparisons:
'Squirrels' by Albrecht Dürer (Albertin Galer, Vienna, Austria)
'Rabbits and Autumn Grasses' – Japanese, Edo Period (British Museum)

Bibliography:
Guy, J and Swallow, G, *The Arts of India* (Victoira & Albert Museum)
Craven, R, *Indian Art* (Thames & Hudson)

6 'The Census at Bethlehem', 1566
Pieter Bruegel (1520–69)

(116 cm × 164 cm)

Musées des Beaux-Arts, Brussels

ABOUT THE ARTIST

Pieter Bruegel was born and grew up in the province of Limburg in Belgium. In his early twenties he went to Antwerp to study art and became a member of the Guild of St Luke. In 1552 he travelled through France to Italy where he met many Italian artists and saw the work of Michaelangelo and Raphael. He made some drawings and paintings of landscapes with towns and filled them with people based on stories from the Bible. He returned from his travels and worked for a man called Jerome Cock, a printmaker. He married and had two sons who were called Pieter and Jan. Because both sons became very good painters like their father, the father became known as Pieter the Elder and the son was called Pieter the Younger. In addition to his own work, Pieter the Younger made copies of a lot of his father's paintings. Jan became well known through working with another artist, Peter Paul Rubens. In addition to the confusion caused by having three men of the same name painting similar pictures, in 1560 Pieter the Elder began to sign his work 'Bruegel' instead of Brueghel. His sons reverted to the earlier spelling and so have an 'h' in their names.

ABOUT THIS WORK

Bruegel was the first person to paint stories from the Bible as if they were happening to real people. Up to this time, the Holy Family had always been portrayed in **icons** or in religious pictures showing them in an idealised way with haloes and angels around them. 'The census', or numbering, here is taking place in a typical 16th century Belgian town.

DISCUSSION POINTS

● It is clearly winter time in the painting. Can you see the people who are walking from one bank of the river to the other? What clues are there to indicate that this is covered in ice and is not a light coloured road? What other clues are there that it is around what we call 'Christmas' time?

● How many birds can you see and what sort are they? Do you put birds in your pictures? Do you choose what sort they will be and make them behave in the ways that they do? For instance, chickens don't fly much because they are too large, but some birds such as ducks and geese do fly. Why is this?

● How long do you think it took the artist to paint this picture? Another of Pieter Bruegel's paintings, 'Children's Games', took several years to paint. In this picture, Bruegel has painted Mary and Joseph wearing the sort of clothes that were common in the town and time in which he lived. Joseph is shown carrying a saw because he was a carpenter by trade. Can you tell what some of the other groups of people are doing?

● This scene illustrates a passage from the Gospel according to St Luke (2:1–5):

At that time the Emperor Augustus ordered a census to be taken throughout the Roman Empire. When this first census took place, Quirinius was the governor of Syria. Everyone, then, went to register himself, each to his own town.

Joseph went from the town of Nazareth in Galilee to the town of Bethlehem in Judaea, the birthplace of King David. Joseph went there because he was a descendant of David.

How was Bruegel able to imagine all these interesting things to put into his picture? Do you look at things around you in this sort of detail?

● Have you spotted the hole in the ice? There is nothing to tell us how it happened, but what are the possible dangers that might arise? Can anyone remember a time when the local river froze? Why do climates vary from one region to another?

ACTIVITIES

Key Stage 1
1(i), 1(vii)

● Look again at the birds in the picture. Some are on the ground or perched on buildings; others are flying, singly or in groups. Try to observe some real birds to see how they behave. It is common for some birds, often sparrows or crows, to perch around the school playground. They fly down as soon as break is over to see what food they can find. Are there any birds around your play area? The children could make drawings of them as they peck at their food. Or your school may have a bird table and the children could put food out for the birds and draw the ones that come.

Key Stage 1
1(i), 1(iii), 1(v), 1(viii)

● Using a viewfinder, isolate small groups of figures within the painting. You will need to make viewfinders of different sizes. Ask the children to 'act' out what is happening in the group and then make drawings of each other in action: for example, they could be pulling a sledge, playing with tops, snowballing, or carrying heavy loads. Find a suitable background where this might be happening and make separate drawings of this. Then the children could make a picture of their own using the information they have gathered in the previous two drawings.

EVALUATION

● In learning more about the lives of people in the past we can begin to appreciate our own in terms of lifestyle, housing, clothing and comfort, and even the influence of politics and beliefs.

● Were the children able to link this painting of events from the past with the fact that Bruegel was painting a picture of events from his own past, from his own reading and knowledge of the Bible?

SUPPORTING INFORMATION

Resources:
– St Luke's Gospel, Chapter 2
– photographs of birds
– birds in the environment

Materials:
viewfinders (card 4 cm × 6 cm)

Topics:
Christmas; the Nativity; children's games

Other works by the artist:
'Harvesters' (Metropolitan Museum, New York)
'Children's Games' (Kunsthistoriches Museum, Vienna, Austria)
'The Wedding Feast' (Kunsthistoriches Museum, Vienna)
'The Fall of Icarus' (Musées des Beaux-Arts, Brussels, Belgium)

Comparisons:
'VE Day 1945' by LS Lowry (Glasgow Art Gallery and Museum) [card 9]
'Christ Carrying the Cross' by Hieronymus Bosch (Kunsthistoriches Museum, Vienna)

Bibliography:
Gibson, M, Bruegel (Tabard)
Morris, J, The Tower of Babel (Dobson)

7 'The Goldfish Bowl' Henri Matisse (1869–1954)

(137.5 cm × 98.4 cm)

Pushkin Museum, Moscow

ABOUT THE ARTIST

Henri Matisse was born in Le Cateau in northern France. His father was a grain merchant and his mother an amateur painter of some talent. After leaving school, he went to work in a solicitors' office and attended drawing classes in his spare time. In 1890, while recovering from an operation he began to paint. He studied seriously, spending hours copying the work of Chardin, Poussin and the old masters in the Louvre, Paris. Later he studied the work of Cézanne and the **Post-Impressionists** and became freer and more colourful in his own painting. His style continued to change and develop throughout his life. For a time he was a member of the group of artists who were called the **Fauves** but he moved on in his own way. He travelled extensively and visited many different countries including Russia, America and North Africa. He worked in a variety of materials over his lifetime, including making murals, stained glass, and sculpture in bronze.

ABOUT THIS WORK

This picture was painted when Matisse was 42. He made other versions of this subject, some of which included a piece of sculpture he had made. It shows his great ability to use colour to convey all the information. The drawing is simplified and pure colours predominate. He obviously enjoyed the distortion in the water of the fishtank and the patterns created by the leaves and flowers.

DISCUSSION POINTS

● What is the centre of interest in this painting? (The answer is the goldfish in the tank.) Look carefully at the picture to see how Matisse has used his paint to show the fish, the water and the plants. What colour background do you think he had to start with? Often when we paint we cover up all of the paper underneath: here, some of it is still showing through the paint.

● The plants in the picture have very contrasting colours and shapes. Can you recognise any of them? (The one in the small pot on the table is often used as a houseplant today; the ones on the lower right are geraniums.)

● Can you work out where the viewer might be standing? On the left of the picture are some railings or a banister. Are we standing on some stairs looking down? How does this affect the shape of the things you can see from there?

● How has the paint been used? Is it thick or thin, or are there areas of both? When you use paint do you think about the thickness? Do you think about where you might want to use it in thick patches or thin, watery ones?

● In contrast to some other paintings in this collection, this one is very large. Using a piece of string, measure it out or draw it on the floor (if not carpeted!) and stick some pieces of paper together to make the shape.

● How many goldfish can you see? Is it four or eight? How is it that things become distorted when we see them through water? Does the curved glass make a difference, or would the fish look the same in an oblong tank?

ACTIVITIES

● Look at the greens that have been used in this painting. Using either oil pastels or powder colour paints, ask the children to make all the greens they can see. They could start with the lightest and work towards the darker ones. Next, make all the colours used for flowers. Are they all pinks, or are there other colours too? Now use the colour chart they have made of the greens, pinks and purples; working in groups of three or four, ask them to make their own painting of a group of plants in the classroom. Make the drawing first in oil pastel or paint and then complete the picture using the colours the children made in their practice.

Key Stage 1
I(i), I(iv), I(v), I(vi)

Key Stage 2
I(i), I(v), I(vi), I(vii)

● Look at the shape of the table in the picture, then at the bottom of the fishtank and then at the top. Although all of these are circles, they are drawn as different shapes. Look carefully at the shape where it meets the table. Then compare that with the shape at the top. See what else they can find out about them.

Key Stage 1
I(viii)

Key Stage 2
I(ix)

● Find a twig or a spoon or straw or anything long and thin. Stand it in a glass half full of water. Ask the children to make careful drawings

Key Stage 1
I(i), I(v)

Key Stage 2
I(i), I(vi)

of what they see, using white chalk on dark paper, or coloured chalks.

● If you are fortunate enough to have goldfish in the school, you could recreate the picture, with some plants placed around the bowl. Ask the children to make their own drawings or painting from the real thing.

EVALUATION

● Were the children able to understand how to draw the fishtank with the fish in it?

● Did they understand about the distortion?

● Were they able to make and appreciate the different greens and did this extend their understanding of colour mixing?

● Did you do the group work? If so, did the children enjoy working on that scale and did they begin to change their ideas of scale in relation to paintings?

SUPPORTING INFORMATION

Resources:
– objects in a glass of water (e.g. spoon or twig)
– fish in aquarium or goldfish in bowl
– house plants

Topics:
reflection and distortion; colour and light; pets

Other works by the same artist:
'La Nappe Rose' (Glasgow Art Gallery)
'The Purple Robe' (Baltimore Museum of Art, USA)
'Still Life with Oysters' (Kunstmuseum, Basle, Switzerland)

Comparisons:
'Almond Twig in a Glass' by Vincent Van Gogh
'Carnations and Clematis in a Crystal Vase' by Edouard Manet (The Louvre, Paris, France)
'Coffee' by Pierre Bonnard (Tate Gallery, London)

Bibliography:
Essers, V, *Henri Matisse* (Taschen)
Flam, J (ed.), *Matisse, a Retrospective* (Macmillan New York)

8 'Carved wooden gates' Yoruba (Nigeria)

(Wooden panel, height 213 cm)

British Museum, London

ABOUT THE CRAFTSPEOPLE

Yoruban carvings and sculptures were made in and around Ife in Nigeria. Ife is near Benin City and the country to the west is called Benin too. The whole of this area of West Africa has a rich tradition of carving in stone and wood, casting in brass and bronze and working with iron and clay. Some of this work dates back to the 12th and 13th centuries.

Benin ivory was found by travellers from Europe – mainly Portuguese, English and Dutch – in the 16th century, but the sculptures did not become known in the West until the British arrived there in 1897. Examples of the Benin Bronzes were brought back and became widely known in Europe. Between 1900 and 1910 they had a great influence on **Cubism** and artists such as Picasso, Matisse and Derain. The Bronzes consist mainly of lifesize human heads, people and animals in relief. It is thought that the Benin craftsmen learnt the complicated skills of lost wax casting from the sculptors of Ife.

ABOUT THIS WORK

Today we think of art as something essentially decorative, to be looked at, enjoyed and discussed. When these doors were made the Yoruban people had no written language and therefore communication was either oral or visual. The carvings show things as they were. The Yoruban craftsmen also made images to do with their beliefs which were bound up with climates, seasons and the harvest.

DISCUSSION POINTS

● Find a map of Africa and pinpoint the area. Look for Nigeria and the river Niger with its vast delta (deposit of silt in the mouth of the estuary). Then find Ife (the area where the Yoruban carving comes from), Benin City and the country of Benin to the west. You might discuss with the children the differences in climate and lifestyle. Find out some more about the region.

● What do you think the people are doing in each of the panels? They all reflect activities that may or may not be linked. As there was no written language in Nigeria when these doors were carved, we cannot be sure. Imagine that the man sitting in the chair (second row, left) is wearing a crown or symbol of authority. Perhaps he was the chief. His visitor (second row, right) must be important because he is being carried. Below the chief could be his warriors. Below them, servants are carrying the chief's belongings and gifts.

● Now look at the figures in the other panels. What do you think they are portraying? Look carefully for clues such as the things they are carrying or wearing, how mothers carry their children and whether the men are free or bound.

● Compare the hats that are being worn. Are men and women wearing the same types?

● What significance might we place on the patterns in the backgrounds of each panel? How many different sorts can you find?

● The decoration at the top of the panel seems to be based on plant forms. What sort of plants grow in this area of the world?

● Can you find the two figures who have 'lost their heads'?

ACTIVITIES

Key Stage 1
I(vii), I(ix), I(i)

Key Stage 2
I(viii), I(x), I(i)

● Using wax crayons or oil pastels on grey or buff sugar paper, ask the children to make drawings of all of the background patterns. They could do this individually or work on it in groups. Then they could use these drawings as a basis for further work in fabric collage, in weaving or in block printing. For any of these three methods the children would first need to be reminded of the craft skills involved and then asked to make a design, based on the patterns on the doors and using a similar range of 'earth' colours. They could go on to invent a variety of designs based on this starting point.

Key Stage 1
I(viii), I(ix)

Key Stage 2
I(ix), I(x)

● Suggest that the children choose one of the figures that they think is most interesting, most unusual or that they like best and make a model of that figure in clay. These doors are very large. Try measuring them against the classroom door. Try to make your clay figure about a third the size, perhaps about 15 centimetres tall.

Key Stage 1
I(ix)

Key Stage 2
I(x)

● For group work, plan and make in clay a small set of free-standing figures based on one of the panels. You could let the children add other figures and things of their own to tell the story of what they think is happening.

● Ask the children to imagine that they find themselves in a country where there is no reading and writing. Challenge them to find a way of communicating some aspect of their daily lives, working in clay not wood. Make the panels about 20 centimetres square.

Key Stage I	**Key Stage 2**
I(ix), I(xi), I(ii)	I(x), I(xii), I(ii)

● You could discuss the packs that are sometimes put aboard space-craft to tell other beings about our world.

Key Stage I	**Key Stage 2**
I(xi), I(ii)	I(xii), I(ii)

EVALUATION

● How did the children respond to the idea of a society for whom painting and sculpture was primarily functional not decorative?

● Were they able to understand some of the differences between the lives of the Yoruban people and our own?

● Did the children enjoy looking at the illustration to try to work out what people were doing and their relationships within the carvings?

● Did they enjoy working in fabric and clay and did they understand how pattern and form can be transferred to another material?

SUPPORTING INFORMATION

Resource:
– map of Africa

Materials:
basic materials for weaving, block printing, clay work

Topics:
African cultures; exploration and discovery; village life in other cultures

Other works:
sculptures and masks from Yoruba and Benin in Nigeria

Comparisons:
sculptures and masks from other cultures e.g. Japan, Oceania, Mexico, Peru
'Les Demoiselles D'Avignon' by Pablo Picasso (Museum of Modern Art, New York)
'Torso in Metal from the Rock Drill' by Jacob Epstein (Tate Gallery, London)

Bibliography:
Herold, E, *African Art* (Hamlyn)
Adam, L, *Primitive Art* (Pelican)
Fagg, W and Plass, M, *African Sculpture* (Dutton Vista)
McLeod, M and Mack, J, *Ethnic Sculpture* (British Museum)

9 'VE Day 1945' L S Lowry (1887–1976)

(78.7 cm × 101.6 cm)

Glasgow Art Gallery and Museum

ABOUT THE ARTIST

Lawrence Stephen Lowry was born in Manchester and lived all his life in the industrial north of England. He learnt how to paint through part-time study at art school in Salford, while working as a rent collector and insurance clerk. He was an eccentric man. He disliked change. He never owned a car or travelled abroad. He lived with his parents until they died and then on his own in a small terraced house.

Nearly all of his work is a celebration of working life in the northern cities of England. Although he painted all his working life, Lowry's work was not fully appreciated until he was in his fifties. In his later years, he became the most popular of all English painters and many people bought prints and postcards of his paintings. He is the only English artist whose work has been celebrated in a popular song: 'He Painted Matchstick Men and Matchstick Cats and Dogs'.

He has been described as 'The English Bruegel'. You may like to compare this painting with 'The Census in Bethlehem' by Pieter Bruegel (card 6).

ABOUT THIS WORK

This painting was made to celebrate 'Victory in Europe' day and shows how people gathered together to celebrate the defeat of Germany towards the end of the Second World War (1939–45). In the city of Salford (Greater Manchester), people gathered in great crowds to sing and dance and cheer the victory. They held parties in the streets and decked the city centre with flags and bunting.

As in many of Lowry's paintings, this great occasion was painted from memory. The work contains scenes of different views of Salford and of buildings from various parts of the city. It does not describe what one part of Salford looked like in May 1945; it is a collection of memories of the city and of the people who lived and worked there.

You can compare this painting with others by Lowry which celebrate such public occasions as 'Good Friday, Daisy Nook' (1946) and 'Agricultural Fair' (1949).

DISCUSSION POINTS

● Lowry described himself as a simple man who used simple means to 'paint what he found'. Can you name the simple range of colours he has used in this painting?

● This painting contains hundreds of different people. Can you see how Lowry has described people by painting just enough of each person to identify them?

● How can you tell that this picture contains scenes from different parts of Salford (in Greater Manchester)? Can you see where the artist has joined the different views together?

● Lowry is famous for the way he described great spaces in his paintings. Can you see how he has made you see right into the distance in this city scene?

● Compare the crowds of people in this painting with those in 'The Census at Bethlehem' by Pieter Bruegel (card 6) and 'The Rout of San Romano' by Paolo Uccello (card 21).

ACTIVITIES

● Ask the children to use a viewfinder to choose a small part of the painting that they particularly like. Make a careful study of the part of the painting.

Key Stage 1	**Key Stage 2**
I(i)	I(i)

● Make a colour chart using crayons and pastels of the colours that Lowry has used:
  – in his painting of buildings
  – in his painting of people
  – in his painting of pavements and streets.

Key Stage 1	**Key Stage 2**
I(vi)	I(vii)

● Make some careful studies of different characters in the painting: dogs, old men, children, women.

Key Stage 1	**Key Stage 2**
I(i)	I(i)

● Make a study of one part of the painting to explain how Lowry has described space by making buildings and people appear to get smaller as they disappear into the distance.

Key Stage 1	**Key Stage 2**
I(viii), I(i)	I(ix), I(i)

● Work in groups to make a painting to celebrate a local event: a town carnival, a village fête, a sporting event etc. You will need to plan this work carefully to share the task within the group.

EVALUATION

● Can you explain why L S Lowry's paintings have been so popular and so much liked by all kinds of people?

● Why do you think he painted people so simply – almost like cartoon characters?

● Does looking at his work help you to see how you can make drawings and paintings of complicated scenes of everyday life?

SUPPORTING INFORMATION

Resources:
– photographs of crowd scenes
– photographs of celebrations

Materials:
viewfinders; magnifying glasses

Topics:
1939–45 World War; city life; celebration

Other works by the same artist:
'Good Friday, Daisy Nook' (Government Art Collection)
'Coming from the Mill' (City of Salford Art Gallery)
'July, the Seaside' (Arts Council Collection)
'The Cripples' (City of Salford Art Gallery)
'Market Scenes, Northern Town' (City of Salford Art Gallery)

Comparisons:
'The Census at Bethlehem' by Pieter Bruegel (Museés des Beaux-Arts, Brussels, Belgium) [card 6]
'The Rout of San Romano' by Paolo Uccello (National Gallery, London) [card 21]
'Boulevard des Capuchines' by Claude Monet (Pushkin Museum, Moscow)

Bibliography:
Levy, M, *The Paintings of L S Lowry* (Jupiter)
Spalding, J, *Lowry* (Herbert/South Bank Board)

10 'Still life with fish' Pablo Picasso (1881–1973)

(Oil paint, 50 cm × 61 cm)

ABOUT THE ARTIST

Picasso was born in Malaga in Spain. His father was a painter and art teacher who encouraged and taught him. Pablo showed very early promise and could draw and paint well from the age of 10. At 14 he went to art school in Barcelona and two years later began exhibiting his work. He moved to Paris in his early twenties where he met and worked with many famous artists who were at the beginning or well into their careers. There were musicians, actors, poets and writers, in addition to people like Matisse and Rousseau (whose work is in this pack), Braque, Derain, Dufy and Utrillo.

Picasso stayed in France for most of the rest of his life. He visited Spain often until the Civil War in 1936 when he was deeply affected by the bombing and slaughter of innocent people. He painted a picture to express his absolute horror at the events. He used only black, white and grey paint in the picture and everything in it conveys outrage and fear. It is called 'Guernica' after the village that was bombed in April 1937. Many people know this painting because it caused such uproar when it was first seen.

Throughout his long life Picasso's beliefs and style of work changed through many moods, movements and influences. He was also very adventurous and his work ranged over many areas, including painting, drawing, sculpture, printmaking, ceramics, ballet and theatre design. His early work has been divided into stages to describe the changes and developments. In 1901–04 came the 'Blue' period where he used sombre, cold colours; 1904–05 the 'Rose' period where pinks crept in and the work was less gloomy. In 1906–07 his painting showed the growing influence of **Cézanne** and the discovery of West African sculpture and the Yoruban carvings (also in this pack). With Georges Braque, he led the Cubist movement which developed out of the previous phase. From then on he was always looking for new ways to show the underlying forms of the things he saw and ways to interpret them which would help others to see these things afresh.

ABOUT THIS WORK

This picture was painted when Picasso had already explored Cubism and was using it to make us look again at familiar things, to see new life and colour in them. He wanted to make the viewer react and appreciate the relationships between the shapes and colours. The very fact that the pan is distorted challenges us to look again. The fish have all the 'essence' of fish without having to be straightforward copies. The lemon is only suggested, but we know it's there. The background of cloth and tabletop enclose the objects and focus our attention on the shapes within.

DISCUSSION POINTS

● What is a 'still life'?
Find other examples in books or on reproductions/postcards to compare with this one. They tell us a lot about how we actually see things. This is a good way of focusing attention on how things look in a group.

● Make up a small arrangement of items on a table top.
Look at the things on the table from three different points of view:
– standing up to look down on it;
– sitting, but still looking down;
– with your chins level with the table top.
From above, the things are seen singly; but as we move down, they begin to overlap and we see them one behind the other. Learning to see the relationships between objects needs practice. It doesn't happen naturally. We need to be able to see groups of things together in order to draw them.

● What sort of fish are these?
Encourage the children to talk about the different sorts of fish they know and where they come from; for example, from fresh or salt water around this country or abroad. If you have an opportunity to look at an aquarium, it would be useful to identify similarities between those tiny fish and the larger ones we see at the fishmongers.

● Try to find a book on this artist's work and look for the painting called 'Les Demoiselles d'Avignon' (1906–07). The figures were painted after Picasso had seen some of the West African sculptures.

● Look at the Yoruban carvings on card 8. Can you find similarities? Picasso had stopped making things look real and began to break up the forms and re-organise them into planes of colour with little light or shadow.

ACTIVITIES

● Try to buy some fish – inexpensive ones will do: herrings, mackerel or even 125 grams of whitebait. Having the real thing makes all the difference to the results and the children will respond in an entirely different way from working with photographs. Give younger children dark paper and oil pastels; older ones can use coloured pencils and cartridge. Ask them to make careful studies of the fish – larger than life to show all the detail (especially if you are using whitebait in which case a magnifying glass is recommended). Ask the children to focus on the fish in this order: first compare the length with the widest part. How narrow does it get at the nose, and at the tail? What shape is the tail? Where are the fish's fins that it uses to swim with? What shape are its eyes, mouth and gills? Has it got a shiny eye? How could you draw this? Then look for the patterns made by scales. What colours can you see? Do they make a pattern too? Draw it lightly at first, then more strongly adding colours, and add the pattern last.

Key Stage 1
1(v), 1(vii), 1(i)

Key Stage 2
1(vi), 1(vii), 1(i)

● Ask the children to work in groups of three or four. They should collect some favourite objects they would like to paint and to make their own 'still life' group. Each person in the group will see the still life from a different point of view so all the drawings will be different too. Use any coloured drawing medium and light or dark sugar paper, whatever will work best with the colours in the still life.

Key Stage 1
1(i), 1(iii)

Key Stage 2
1(i), 1(iv)

● Find a frying pan and use charcoal, chalk and grey sugar paper to make drawings of it. Ask the children to look hard at the shape and try to show what they can see of the inside as well as the shape of the whole pan.

Key Stage 1
1(v), 1(i)

Key Stage 2
1(vi), 1(i)

EVALUATION

● Did the children understand that Picasso was a brilliant draughtsman but chose to explore other ways of representing what he saw?

● If you were able to look at other examples of Picasso's work, did the children understand that an artist can be influenced by many others?

● Did they understand that all of us benefit from seeing and enjoying lots of different sorts and styles of painting?

● Did the children appreciate that it isn't always necessary to try to paint things to look exactly as we see them to make a good picture?

SUPPORTING INFORMATION

Resources:
- photographs/pictures of different kinds of fish
- fish from the local fishmonger e.g. herring, whitebait, mackerel
- large frying pan
- selection of still life objects

Topics:
food; the sea

Other works by the artist:
'Glass Bottle and Guitar 1912' (Tate Gallery, London)
'The Family of Saltimbanques' (National Gallery, Washington DC, USA)
'Paulo as Harlequin' (Picasso Museum, Paris, France)

Comparisons:
'Still life with Mackerels, Lemons and Tomatoes' by Vincent Van Gogh
 (Oscar Reinhart Collection, USA)
'La Jalousie' by Juan Gris (Tate Gallery, London)
'Still Life, 1925' by Georges Braque (Tate Gallery)

Bibliography:
Raboff, E, *Art for Children: Picasso* (Benn)
Measham, T, *Picasso and his World* (Ward Lock)
Boone, D, *Picasso* (Bracken Books)
Walther, I, *Pablo Picasso* (Taschen) and *Picasso and the Cubists*
 (Bloomsbury Books)

11 'Autumn Leaves'
John Everrett Millais
(1829–96)

(104.3 cm × 74 cm)

City of Manchester Art Galleries

ABOUT THE ARTIST

Millais was one of the founder members of a school of painters called the **Pre-Raphaelite Brotherhood**. Rosetti, Burne-Jones, William Morris and Holman Hunt also belonged to the group. They were influenced by the work done in Italy in the 12th and 13th centuries – particularly the **Sienese School** who were succeeded by Raphael, Michaelangelo and Leonardo da Vinci who were some of the notable painters of the Renaissance. Millais won a Gold Medal and exhibited at the Royal Academy in London when he was only 17. Some of his early work centred on religious stories; later, he worked on more popular story-telling themes.

ABOUT THIS WORK

This picture was painted in Millais' more popular period and describes an event from everyday life. The real size of this painting is, like others in the set, very different. It is almost twice as big in reality as you see it here. Other paintings by Millais include 'The Blind Girl' (City of Birmingham Museum and Art Gallery), 'Ophelia' (National Gallery) and 'The Boyhood of Raleigh' painted when Millais lived in Devon.

DISCUSSION POINTS

● What time of the year does this picture show us and what is happening?

● Look at the colours. Which ones do you notice first? If you made a painting like this, what colours would you need to use most and least? Would you need any blue? If you do, what sort of blue does it need to be?

● The colours used for the girls' dresses are very dark, with one exception. How might you make the dark colours and still be able to show all of the detail? In the 19th century when this picture was painted, did children wear long dresses all day and every day? How would you feel if you had to wear a long dress all the time?

- Is the pile of leaves actually a bonfire? How can we tell? What memories have you got of bonfires? How recently did you see leaves looking dry like this?

- Do you think the girls are sisters? If you do, what makes you think so and can you tell how old they might be? Look at the details in the painting of the leaves. Each one shows up in its own colours. The spaces in between are dark. How might this influence the way you might make your own paintings?

- Have you ever drawn or painted a bonfire? Perhaps you did a painting near Guy Fawkes night? Did you do it before the day of the bonfire or afterwards when your memory was fresh? Which way do you think would help you to make a better drawing or painting?

ACTIVITIES

Key Stage I
I (x), I (iii)

Key Stage 2
I (xi), I (iv)

- Ask the children to make a collection of leaves. Suggest they look for some that are yellow, some red, as many different browns as they can find and ones with more than one colour. Spread the leaves out and have a discussion about the variety of colours. Then look at the shapes. Which come from bushes, which from trees? Do big leaves come from big trees?

- Work with wax crayons on buff or brown sugar paper. Ask the children to practise on a small piece of paper and try to match the colours of three of the leaves. Choose the ones which have the shapes they like best. Make sure the crayons are used thickly enough to cover the paper and that the colours are well blended. Now ask the children how they would have drawn this picture and ask them to make their own version.

Key Stage I
I (vi), I (i)

Key Stage 2
I (vii), I (i)

- For observation work, use oil pastels on dark brown or black sugar paper. Begin by practising with the pastels and making samples of the colours they can see in three of the leaves. Ask the children to choose their favourite leaf and use a magnifying glass to view it more closely. Make a drawing at least three times the size of the leaf so that they can show detail.

Key Stage I
I (viii), I (i), I (iii)

Key Stage 2
I (ix), I (i), I (iv)

- Use powder colour with white added to make it show up on dark paper. Look at the pile of leaves and add some items of your own – a trug (shallow basket), gardening gloves, hand fork or other gardening tools. Ask the children to make a painting of their own using this as a starting point.

EVALUATION

● Did the children expand their vocabulary through describing the leaves, colours and shapes?

● Did they understand how to work well on dark paper?

SUPPORTING INFORMATION

Resources:
— collection of autumn leaves
— magnifying glasses
— gardening tools and objects

Topics:
autumn; families; colour and light

Other works by the artist:
'The Woodman's Daughter' (Guildhall Art Library, London)
'Christ in the House of his Parents' (Tate Gallery, London)
'The Blind Girl' (Birmingham City Art Gallery)
'Ophelia' (Tate Gallery, London)
'The Boyhood of Raleigh' (Tate Gallery, London)

Comparisons:
'The Last of England' by Ford Maddox Brown (Birmingham City Art Gallery) [card 15]
'The Travelling Companions' by Augustus Egg (Birmingham City Art Gallery)
'Amy' by Arthur Hughes (Birmingham City Art Gallery)
'Pretty Baa Lambs' by Ford Maddox Brown (Birmingham City Art Gallery)

Bibliography:
Reynolds, G, Victorian Painting (Guild Publishing)
Hilton, T, The Pre-Raphaelites (Thames & Hudson)
Rose, A, The Pre-Raphaelites (Phaidon)

12 'Mr and Mrs Clark and Percy', 1970–01
David Hockney (1937–)
(Acrylic on canvas, 214 cm × 305 cm)

ABOUT THE ARTIST

David Hockney was born in Bradford in 1937. He is perhaps the most popular of all English contemporary artists. He has appeared many times on television, talking about the work he makes. He studied at Bradford School of Art and then at the Royal College of Art. He is a very versatile artist and has worked successfully as painter, graphic designer, theatre designer, illustrator and photographer.

Nearly all his work is based upon his own experiences in life. He has drawn, painted and photographed his friends, their houses and possessions and places he has visited and where he enjoys living.

Amongst his best known works are his portrait drawings and paintings of figures in interiors, his paintings of swimming pools and his designs for operatic productions.

ABOUT THIS WORK

This painting is of Ossie Clark, the fashion designer, with his wife Celia and their cat Percy. It is a 'double portrait', like the painting 'Mr and Mrs Andrews' by Thomas Gainsborough which was painted 200 years earlier and which is also in this collection.

It is a very big painting – you need to measure it out on the wall of the classroom to realise its size. David Hockney made lots of small drawings of Mr and Mrs Clark and took many photographs of them before he worked on the painting. They posed for him for many hours in his studio. He worked on the painting for seven months and he painted and re-painted Ossie Clark's head 12 times before he was satisfied with it!

In the painting, the figures are nearly life-size and David Hockney has said that he made the painting this size so that anyone looking at it would feel as though they were actually in the room with Mr and Mrs Clark.

DISCUSSION POINTS

● People 'pose' for a portrait painting like this in the same way as they pose for a photograph. Have you ever posed for a photograph?

Who are Mr and Mrs Clark looking at? Who are Mr and Mrs Andrews looking at in the painting by Thomas Gainsborough (card 19)? Compare these with family photographs, school photographs or photographs of special occasions such as weddings. How do people pose themselves to look at their best on these occasions?

● What kind of people are Ossie and Celia Clark? What can you tell about them from their house, their possessions and the clothes they wear? Write a short description of each of them.

● Look at other portrait paintings and compare them with photographs of people. How does a portrait painting tell us more about people than a photograph?

● Can you see where you could divide this painting to make two separate pictures – one of Mr Clark and the other of Mrs Clark? Which half do you like best?

● David Hockney has described this as a very difficult painting to make because the light is coming from the window in the centre. Can you see how he has painted the light and the shadows to show where the light is coming from?

ACTIVITIES

● Use this painting to encourage the children to work 'like an artist'. Ask them to choose two people from their family and friends:
 – mother and father
 – neighbours
 – uncle and aunt
 – brother and sister
 – grandparents etc.

Key Stage 1	Key Stage 2
I(vii), I(viii), I(i), I(ii), I(iii)	I(viii), I(ix), I(i), I(ii), I(iv)

● Collect photographs of their chosen couple. Make drawings from observation or memory of the couple's favourite room, possessions, clothes they wear for special occasions, etc.

● Encourage the children to make several 'practice' drawings of different ways in which they might arrange their painting to 'present' their couple as attractively as possible.

Key Stage 1	Key Stage 2
I(iv), I(ii)	I(v), I(ii)

● Make a painting of a 'double portrait'.

Key Stage 1	Key Stage 2
I(vii), I(viii), I(iii)	I(viii), I(ix), I(iv)

EVALUATION

● Have the children understood how carefully you need to plan and prepare for making a painting of this kind?

58

● Do they appreciate the difference between a photograph of a person and a portrait painting?

SUPPORTING INFORMATION

Resources:
- family photographs
- wedding photographs
- photographs of relatives and friends (interiors)
- collections of favourite personal possessions

Topics:
me and my family; clothes; houses

Other works by the artist:
'A Bigger Splash' (Tate Gallery, London)
'My Parents and Myself' (collection of the artist)
'Portrait of Sir David Webster' (Royal Opera House, Covent Garden, London)

Comparisons:
'Mr and Mrs Andrews' by Thomas Gainsborough (National Gallery, London) [card 19]
'The Marriage of Giovanni Arnolfini' by Jan van Eyck (National Gallery)
'The Ambassadors' by Hans Holbein the Younger (National Gallery)

Bibliography
Stangos, N (ed.), *David Hockney on David Hockney* (Guild Publishing)
Compton, S (ed.), *British Art of the Twentieth Century* (Prestel)

13 'Landscape near Mont Majour', 1888 Vincent Van Gogh (1853–90)

(Pen, reed pen and black chalk, 49 cm × 61 cm)

British Museum, London

ABOUT THE ARTIST

Vincent Van Gogh was one of the most remarkable and celebrated artists of all time. In his short working life he made many paintings like 'Sunflowers', 'Bedroom at Arles' and 'Starry Night' which are familiar to everyone through reproductions and postcards of his work.

He lived an intense and troubled life. Vincent began his working life as an art dealer with a family firm and then unsuccessfully attempted to be a lay preacher and missionary to a poor mining community in Belgium. He did not begin to work as an artist until he was 27. For the next ten years he lived and worked in poverty, helped only by an allowance from his brother Theo, to whom he wrote a famous series of letters about his paintings.

He worked for a short time in Paris where he was influenced by the work of the **Impressionist** painters and their vibrant use of colour. Nearly all of his best known work was made during the last two years of his life, at Arles and St Remy in France. Here he painted in a frenzy of activity, working long hours and often going without proper food in order to buy the painting materials he needed. During these last years he suffered a series of mental illnesses. Vincent Van Gogh took his own life in July 1890.

ABOUT THIS WORK

This drawing is one of the many hundreds that Van Gogh made in preparation for his paintings. He spent many years learning how to draw. He began by copying drawings by other artists whose work he admired, such as Rembrandt and Millet. He was also influenced by the drawing techniques used by the Impressionist painters and the drawings that he saw in Japanese prints in Paris.

He made this drawing using a pen with a steel nib, a pen cut from a reed (like a quill pen) and black chalk. The drawing, like his paintings, is full of energy and movement. He has used the different drawing materials to make different kinds of marks and patterns which describe the landscape.

In making these drawings of landscapes, people and places Van Gogh was gaining the knowledge and understanding that was to help him paint so vividly and directly from his environment.

DISCUSSION POINTS

● Can you see where the artist has used different drawing materials in this work? (The artist used a pen with a steel nib, a reed pen and black chalk.)

● How many different kinds of marks and patterns can you see in the drawing?

● Compare this drawing with one of Van Gogh's landscape paintings. Can you see anything that is the same in them both?

● How does the artist show space in this landscape drawing? Compare this style with the way that L S Lowry has made you see right into the distance in his painting 'VE Day 1945' (card 9).

● Try to find some reproductions of other artists' drawings. Compare their methods of drawing with Van Gogh's.

ACTIVITIES

Key Stage 2
1(i), 1(vi), 1(ix)

● Ask the children to fold a piece of A4 paper so that it makes eight sections. Try to find in the drawing eight different ways that Van Gogh has used marks to make patterns and textures. Using a fine brush with ink or watercolour, copy these different patterns in the eight sections of the paper.

Key Stage 2
1(i), 1(vi)

● Using a viewfinder, find three different kinds of detail in the drawing: trees, fields, people etc. Make careful studies of these. The children may need to use biro and conte crayons, as well as brush with inks, to make sure of the fine detail.

Key Stage 2
1(i), 1(vi), 1(viii)

● Look for interesting views from windows around your school. The children may find it easier to use a window pane as a viewfinder, or make a frame in the window using brown gummed tape. Ask them to make small studies of views using pencils and biros until they find one that they really like. Then make a careful drawing of the chosen view using some of Van Gogh's drawing methods to describe the different patterns and textures that they can see.

EVALUATION

● Has the way in which you see and draw the local landscape been changed by making a drawing using some of Vincent Van Gogh's methods?

● When you have looked at a number of Van Gogh's paintings, can you begin to tell what kind of man he was?

SUPPORTING INFORMATION

Materials:
viewfinders; A4 paper folded into eight sections; window viewfinders (gummed paper frames on windows)

Topics:
farming and harvest

Other works by the artist:
'Vincent's Bedroom at Arles' (Rijksmuseum, Amsterdam)
'Harvest Landscape, 1888' (Rijksmuseum, Amsterdam)
'Chair with a Pipe' (Tate Gallery, London)
'Farms near St Auvers' (Tate Gallery)
'Starry Night' (Museum of Modern Art, New York)

Comparisons:
'Gleaning Fields' by Samuel Palmer (Tate Gallery)
'Harvest Le Pouldu' by Paul Gauguin (Tate Gallery)
'The Harvest' by Raoul Dufy (Tate Gallery)

Bibliography:
Mascheroni, H (ed.), *Vincent Van Gogh* (Bloomsbury)
Measham, T, *Van Gogh and his World* (Ward Lock)
Venezia, M, *Van Gogh* (Franklin Watts)
Amarin, C, *Vincent Van Gogh* (Art Line Editions)
Petrie, B, *Van Gogh* (Tiger Books)
Bernard, B, *Vincent by Himself* (Orbis)

14 'The Spinning Top', circa 1751–57
Torii Kiyohiro

(Wood block, 43.2 cm × 30 cm)

British Museum, London

ABOUT THE ARTIST

Torii stands for a school of printmakers started by the Torii family. So this group of artists all had names which began with 'Torii' followed by their own names. Kiyohiro was one of the finest of the third generation of artists at a time in the development of Japanese printmaking when two-colour prints could be made. These were called 'benizuri-e' (pink printed pictures). The pink dye was obtained from the safflower. Later, in the 1760s, blocks with as many as five colours could be made. Finally, in 1765, full colour prints were achieved. At this time in Edo (the old name for Tokyo), Kabuki and No theatre was very important and Kiyohiro's favourite subjects were actors and fashionable ladies.

Printmaking was a team activity at this time. The artist made a drawing on thin white paper and it was stuck down on to a wood block. The engraver then cut it out and the picture was printed in black. The artist then coloured the print and blocks were made for the two colours and carefully printed.

ABOUT THIS WORK

The young man, with the distinctive chequered pattern round his neck, is known to be a famous actor called Sanogawa Ichimatsu. He is watching the two boys playing with their tops. The writing tells us the two boys are brothers. The man is wearing a sword and from it hang what were thought to be letters from his admirers.

DISCUSSION POINTS

● The height of this print is about the same size as the card. If you imagine it that size you can get a good idea of just how fine the detail is. The composition of the figures is based on a triangle and the figures fill the space without overcrowding it. All of the movement and interest is centred in the middle with the three figures looking inward. What are all three faces looking at? Our eyes are guided round the picture by the lines the artist has used.

● The figures are all wearing clothes that were fashionable at the time. Look carefully and note the type of sleeves that the loose jackets have. The three figures are wearing belts of different designs and thicknesses. Now look at their shoes. Do people wear shoes like this nowadays? Why do you think that one has platforms? Do you know if this was common in Japan at the time?

● This picture was printed from three wood blocks. Look carefully to see how fine the lines are. How were the engravers able to make the match between the three blocks so perfect? The two colours are soft and work well together. The printers had to use natural dyes. What natural dyes do you know about? It's fun to try some out.

● If you look at the longest column of Japanese writing in the centre of the print you will see there are five characters. From top to bottom, the third and fourth are Kiyohiro's signature; the whole column says: 'By the brush of Kiyohiro'. The two square seals are the date and censor marks and the writing above them describes the people shown in the print.

ACTIVITIES

● Ask the children to make some drawings – using wax or pencil crayons on light coloured paper – of some of the patterns they can see. Restrict them to two colours and black. Make the shapes just large enough to cut into a potato. Remember that all prints come out the opposite way round; while this needn't spoil a pattern, it will make a difference. To make the patterns reflect the style of this print, try to keep to similar colours. Ask them to cut their potato blocks and print them, on light coloured paper, overlapping the prints to make them look like the Japanese one.

Key Stage 2
1(i), 1(iv), 1(viii), 1(x)

● Woodblock carving takes a long time to learn but you can achieve an idea of how it was done by pressing into a thick sheet of card with the back of a craft knife or by using 'poly' press or print – the same type of material that is used by supermarkets to pack their meat (this makes a good free alternative). Make some simple line drawings of tops, hoops, balls, dice or other things we play with. Use these drawings to make a simple print drawing into the block with a pencil or biro.

Key Stage 2
1(i), 1(iv), 1(x)

● Look again at the patterns. Stick fine string on to stiff card to make a simple block to print with. Use only black printing ink and make several prints. Let them dry thoroughly. Then hand colour these in the way that the early Japanese did using only two colours but trying out different combinations of colours.

Key Stage 2
General requirements,
1(i), 1(iv), 1(v)

Key Stage 2

I(i), I(v), I(vi)

● Ask the children to use a fine brush and some black ink to try out some Japanese writing. They could copy the characters in the print. The secrets of success are practise, control and a varied pressure on the brush to make thick and thin lines.

EVALUATION

● Were the children able to understand how these prints were made and appreciate that only two colours and black were used?

● Did they enjoy a new method of pattern making?

● Were they able to relate the facts about these artists and understand that they were the ancestors of the present-day Japanese who are so efficient and ingenious at manufacturing and so competent at design?

● If they experimented with Japanese writing, did they come to realise what enormous control and skill it takes?

SUPPORTING INFORMATION

Resources:
- spinning tops
- hoops
- dice
- other toys

Materials:
printmaking materials; polypress; craft knives; cardboard; fine string; inks

Topics:
games and toys; dress; the Far East

Other works by the artist:
'The Letter in the Wind' (British Museum)
'Six Actors under Umbrellas' (British Museum)

Comparisons:
Other Japanese printmakers: Torii Kiyoshige, Okumura Masanobu, Toshusai Sharaku, Katasushika Hokusai, Ando Hiroshige etc. (British Museum)
'Children's Games' by Pieter Bruegel (Kunsthistoriches Museum, Vienna)
'In the Park' by L S Lowry

Bibliography:
Smith, L, *Ukiyoe, Images of Unknown Japan* (British Museum)
Hajek, L, *Japanese Graphic Art* (Galley Press)
Kobayashi, T, *Great Japanese Art* (Sawers)

15 'The Last of England',
1852–55
Ford Maddox Brown
(1821–93)

(Oil on canvas, 85 cm × 73 cm)

Birmingham City Museum and Art Gallery

ABOUT THE ARTIST

Ford Maddox Brown was born in France, trained as an artist in Belgium and came to work in England in his early twenties. He was a serious and hard working man. Many of his early paintings were based upon historical and Biblical events and stories. He was a careful and painstaking painter. He worked on 'The Last of England' for over three years and it took him four weeks to paint the red ribbons to the bonnet that the woman in the painting is wearing.

Although he was never a member, he knew those painters who belonged to the Pre-Raphaelite Brotherhood – such as John Everett Millais who painted 'Autumn Leaves', which is also in this collection (11). Like them, he wanted to paint very realistic pictures that were true to life: 'I have tried to render this scene as it would appear!' He also wanted his paintings to have a message, to make people think about what life was like for the people in his paintings.

His most popular paintings were 'Work' and 'The Last of England'. These are called '**genre**' paintings because they describe everyday life at a particular time. They were popular because people at the time both admired the great skill with which they were painted and could associate events and stories in the paintings with happenings in their own lives.

ABOUT THIS WORK

Ford Maddox Brown was inspired to make this painting after a visit to Gravesend to say farewell to a friend who was emigrating to Australia. He was affected by the sadness of the occasion: so many people in this country had to emigrate to the Colonies or to the United States of America to escape poverty here and to try to make a new life for themselves abroad.

The models for the figures in the painting were the artist himself and his wife, Emma. Because he was so determined to get the right cold and gloomy atmosphere in the work, he painted most of it out of doors on dull, cold days. His wife had to sit for him shivering in the cold.

In this work, Ford Maddox Brown describes in great detail what it was like to be huddled together with hundreds of other people on board ship and to be embarking upon a long and dangerous journey.

DISCUSSION POINTS

● This painting is nearly round. Can you see how the artist carefully 'composed' the painting by placing curves within the circle? If you make a tracing from a postcard of this painting you will see how the figures are arranged within the circle.

● Ford Maddox Brown made this painting after saying farewell to a friend who was emigrating to Australia. There are lots of detail in this painting which give clues about what it was like to make this kind of voyage. What was the weather like? What were the different people thinking about? Why are there cabbages hanging from the netting in the foreground?

ACTIVITIES

Key Stage 2
I(i), I(v)

● This painting is full of interesting detail. Make a group study of different parts of the painting. Use viewfinders to find and select details of hands, faces, clothes, parts of the ship, the landscape beyond, etc.

Key Stage 2
I(i), I(vi), I(vii)

● Look at the way the artist has used colour to describe the surface and texture of clothes. Using crayons and pastels on grey paper, ask the children to make careful studies of some of these.

Key Stage 2
I(iv), I(v)

● You can tell that the husband and wife in the painting are anxious about the forthcoming voyage both by the expression on their faces and by the way the wife clutches her husband's hand. Look at other paintings or photographs of people who are worried or under stress. Make some studies from these to show how that worry is reflected in their facial expressions. Using a mirror, ask the children to make drawings of their own face looking worried or sad.

Key Stage 2
I(i), I(v), I(vi),
I(viii), I(ix)

● Make a painting of two or three people huddled together, sheltering from the wind and rain. Make preliminary studies and drawings of children in the class who are suitably dressed and posed.

EVALUATION

● Can you explain how Ford Maddox Brown has used this painting to make us feel concerned about the plight of people emigrating to another country?

SUPPORTING INFORMATION

Resources:
– postcard reproductions of 'The Last of England'
– photographs of people who are worried or unhappy

Materials:
viewfinders; tracing paper; mirrors

Topics:
families; journeys; transport

Other works by the artist:
'Pretty Baa Lambs' (City of Birmingham Art Gallery)
'Work' (City of Birmingham Art Gallery)
'An English Autumn Afternoon' (City of Birmingham Art Gallery)

Comparisons:
'Autumn Leaves' by John Everett Millais (City of Manchester Art Gallery)
   [card 11]
'The Doctor' by Luke Fildes (Tate Gallery, London)
'The Hopeless Dawn' by Frank Bramley (Tate Gallery)

Bibliography:
Reynolds, G, *Victorian Painting* (Guild Publishing)
Hilton, T, *The Pre-Raphaelites* (Thames & Hudson)
Rose, A, *The Pre-Raphaelites* (Phaidon)

16 'Southwold', 1937
Stanley Spencer
(1891–1959)

(81 cm × 50.8 cm)

City of Aberdeen Art Gallery and Museums Collections

ABOUT THE ARTIST

Stanley Spencer was born into a large family at Cookham-on-Thames in Berkshire. His father was a musician and teacher and his mother took the family to chapel every Sunday where they learnt about religion. Stanley Spencer related this in his paintings to the everyday life of Cookham which then was a comparatively isolated village with few distractions. He trained as a painter, mainly at the Slade School, though he was never influenced in his choice of subject matter. He painted in and around his home until the First World War began in 1914. He joined up and after working in an army hospital was sent to Mesopotamia. After the war he was officially commissioned as a war artist to record some of the things he had seen. Later in life, he became very disillusioned but continued to paint religious scenes set in his beloved Cookham, the countryside, the war, his friends and himself.

ABOUT THIS WORK

This picture was painted in 1937 – some 12 years after Stanley Spencer got married in a little village close by. It shows a typical beach scene in the years before package holidays, when fewer families could afford to go away each year. Nowadays, beaches get very crowded but in this picture the people are in little groups. It looks as if the artist has recorded the scene just as he might have seen it looking down from the promenade.

DISCUSSION POINTS

● What time of day do you think it is in the picture? What clues can you find to help you? Some of these suggestions may help:
  – Which direction is the light coming from?
  – Is a strong or gentle wind blowing? The intensity of colour and subtle tones will help you to decide.
  – Are these the short shadows of midday or the longer ones of late afternoon?

— Does it feel hot, warm or beginning to get cool?

● Look at the area of pebbles. How do we know they are getting further away? Is it only the size that changes or is it the colour and tone too? What colours has the artist chosen to paint the water and the waves? Look at the colours of the water in a pond or stream or river nearby. Does it only look blue when there is a blue sky? Does it ever look blue?

● How many deckchairs can you see? Some of them are partly hidden. There are different colours and they are arranged in groups. Do you think they would be comfortable to sit in? People are reading papers, dozing, chatting and watching the sea. Remember that this picture was painted some time ago. How might some beaches look different now?

● Going across the picture is a clothes line for hanging wet costumes and towels on. Can you see the shed side and the windbreak on the left and the line of posts on the right? The lines of this painting are strong. They focus our attention and carry our eyes round the picture.

● The flapping towel on the line looks as if it is actually flapping in the wind. How has the artist used colour to achieve this?

ACTIVITIES

● Ask the children to isolate a patch of pebbles with a viewfinder. Look carefully at the variations in colour. Using powder colour and dark paper, ask the children to make the colours they can see. They will need to use more white to make the paler colours show up on the dark paper. Remember, the pebbles are different sizes in different parts of the picture. You could use the same technique to paint the sea and the waves. After this, the children could go on to paint their own beach picture, either following a visit to the seaside or recreating a miniature seaside scene in the classroom using toys and 'fish tank' gravel.

Key Stage 2
1(i), 1(vii)

● If you can find a deckchair similar to one of these, set it up in the classroom and ask the children to look at it from different angles. Use grey sugar paper, cut to A4, and white and coloured chalks. Begin by looking at the spaces created through the legs of the deckchair – big, little; squares and triangles. Ask the children to draw these spaces in white chalk. Next, try to match the wood – draw it in buff or grey. Finally, use the coloured chalks to draw the fabric. Make several quick sketches from different angles. After some practise, use larger paper to make a more detailed study.

Key Stage 2
1(i), 1(vi)

Key Stage 2
1(i), 1(v)

● Look at the towels and costumes on the line. You could set up a similar line across a corner of the room. Using oil pastels and dark paper, the children could make drawings of them.

Key Stage 2
1(i), 1(vii)

● There are very distinct shadows in this picture. If you go out into the playground on a bright day, look carefully at some shadows. Talk about or make some colours to show the difference between a patch of colour in sunlight and shadow.

EVALUATION

● Were the children able to get a sense of the past from this painting and did they appreciate how long ago it was painted?

● Did they understand the way that tones have been used to create the atmosphere of soft light and movement in the picture?

● Could the children appreciate that shadows are not made by adding black paint to a colour? But when they studied them carefully were they able to see that they are actually other tones of the colour?

SUPPORTING INFORMATION

Resources:
– viewfinders
– collection of pebbles
– deckchair
– washing line with towels and swimming costumes

Topics:
colour and light; families; the sea

Other works by the artist:
'Greenhouses and Gardens' (Hull City Museum and Art Galleries)
'Swan Upping at Cookham' (Tate Gallery, London)
'Shipbuilding on the Clyde' (Imperial War Museum, London)
'Gardens in the Pound, Cookham' (Leeds City Art Gallery)

Comparison:
'Boulogne Sands' by Philip Wilson Steer (Tate Gallery, London)
'On the Beach' by Laura Knight (Laing Art Gallery, Newcastle on Tyne)
'Lytham Pier' by L S Lowry (Crane Kalman Gallery, London)

Bibliography:
Robinson, D, *Stanley Spencer* (Phaidon)
Express Art Books, *Stanley Spencer* (Beaverbrook Press)
Compton, S (ed.), *British Art in the Twentieth Century* (Prestel)
Robinson, D, *Stanley Spencer: Visions from a Berkshire Village* (Phaidon)

17 Detail from folio 250v of the Book of Kells showing ornamented words, late 7th or early 8th century

(Vellum, 33 cm × 24 cm)

Trinity College, Dublin

ABOUT THE ARTISTS

The origins of this book are uncertain but it is thought to have originated in Ireland. It bears a strong resemblance to an equally famous book called the Lindisfarne Gospels in Northumbria. These beautiful books were written by monks who spent all their days copying Bibles and other holy scripts. Every monastery needed to have their own books to study and to use for teaching other monks and clergy. Prior to the invention of the printing press in the mid-15th century, the monks themselves did all the work. They used a mixture of old Latin and the 'Vulgate' (St Jerome's translation of the Bible commonly accepted by the end of the 6th century). The Book of Kells consists mainly of the four Gospels, with some preliminary chapters. Many scholars have studied it and believe that it is the work of three monks judging by the slight variation in styles.

ABOUT THIS WORK

A manuscript is called 'illuminated' if it is decorated with gold and silver. It was written on vellum (which is the specially prepared skins of sheep and calves) using soot, lamp black, or iron gall (sulphate of iron and oak apples) mixed with gum and water for ink. The colours were made from animal, vegetable and mineral substances.

DISCUSSION POINTS

● The Book of Kells consists mainly of the Gospels. Each of the four saints have their own symbols: St Matthew's is a man, St Mark's a lion, St Luke's a calf and St John's an eagle. These symbols occur often in the Book of Kells. Can you find any examples of these?

● This page is from St Luke's Gospel, Chapter 15, verse 10. The first line of the text is from the previous verse; the second line, including the capitals, reads (in Latin): 'Ita dico uobis' (Likewise, I say unto you). The fifth line reads: 'Ait autem' (And he said). This is how the monks of 1200 years ago wrote the parables. Find a bible and read the stories. Then look at this picture again. Can you pick out any other letters or words?

● What strange creatures can you pick out in the illustration? How many can you find? How many look most like birds, animals or snakes? Look carefully at the patterns that link the creatures together. Can you see how they twine over and under each other? Have you noticed the tiny dots? Can you find other examples of this type of decoration? There is little actual evidence of this period to be found but these same patterns occur on jewellery and weapons made at the same time.

● The monks wrote on vellum made from animal skins. This limited the size of the books that could be made. They also worked in what were called folios, that is, one piece of vellum folded in two and written on both sides (four sides of writing). These beautiful books also had covers made from wooden boards covered in leather and richly decorated with gold and jewels. How are books made today? Find some that are inexpensive and compare them with some that are made to last.

ACTIVITIES

Key Stage 2
1(i), 1(v)

● Ask the children to look at how the letters are written and where the thick and thin lines of the letters are. Using pens with italic nibs and black ink, try to copy some of the letters. The children will need to practise until they can keep the pen nib at the right angle to get the thick and thin strokes in the right places. Then choose something to write, either from St Luke's Gospel or from a favourite poem. Write it out in this type of script.

Key Stage 2
1(i), 1(v)

● Using their own names, ask the children to design a panel on A4 size paper used 'landscape' (so that the name will fit in from one end to the other), with an illuminated letter for the first one. They could draw out the letters faintly in pencil first and then write the letters in black or coloured ink (if it's available) with their italic pens. Then they could paint the capital letter with watercolours. They could use metallic paint or wax crayons, if you have any.

Key Stage 2
1(i), 1(vii)

● Have they identified any of the creatures? The first activity here would be for the children to make simple colour charts of the colours the monks have used in their decorations; then to make a copy either of the head of one of the birds, snakes or animals, or a copy of the whole of one creature. Use A3 or A4 paper and make the copy in pencil first and then colour it. If they choose a whole creature they may need some very odd shaped paper!

- Look at the intricately woven patterns. Where do we see patterns like these? Find some baskets, loosely woven fabrics, plaited things or straps on shoes and make some drawings to show how the canes or threads move over and under each other.

Key Stage 2

1(iv), 1(v), 1(vi)

EVALUATION

- Were the children able to understand how old this book is and that it is one of few pieces of actual first-hand evidence that we have of life at that time? Could they imagine what different lives were lived with so few distractions from the basic life of work and survival?

- Did they respond to the intricate Celtic designs and enjoy copying and making them?

- Did looking at and working from this one page stimulate the children into wanting to see more of this book and other illuminated manuscripts?

SUPPORTING INFORMATION

Resources:
- the Gospel according to St Luke
- woven and plaited objects: fabrics, baskets etc.
- books with different bindings
- examples of lettering from different times and cultures

Materials:
pens with italic nibs

Topics:
communications (printing); lettering and typography; book making; the Celts

Other works:
other illuminations from The Book of Kells

Comparisons and bibliography:
Longman, J and Cazanes, R, *Trés Riches Heures* (Thames & Hudson)
Backhouse, J, *The Lindisfarne Gospels* (Phaidon)
Backhouse, J, *The Bedford Hours* (British Library, London)
Harthan, J, *Books of Hours* (Thames & Hudson)
Payne, A, *Medieval Beasts* (British Library)

18 'Goggle Head', 1967
Dame Elisabeth Frink
(1931–)
(Bronze, 60.2 cm high)

ABOUT THE ARTIST

Dame Elisabeth Frink is the daughter of an army officer. After her formal education, she went to art school to study painting and some months after beginning the course decided she was much more interested in sculpture. During this time, like Gwen John, she worked as a model at Chelsea School of Art. Late in the 1950s, her work was exhibited and she went to live in France. She felt this experience greatly strengthened her work.

Her sculpture has centred on figures – heads, and a variety of animals, all made in either plaster or bronze. Her latest work is concerned with horses. She was made a Dame in 1982 for her services to British sculpture and has received an honorary degree from St Hilda's College, Oxford, and Newnham College, Cambridge. Her work can be seen from time to time at the Yorkshire Sculpture Park, Bretton Hall, Yorkshire, and in a variety of exhibitions round the country.

ABOUT THIS WORK

The goggle heads are a series of sculptures portraying power, strength and menace. The original head for the series was modelled on the President of Algeria, Houari Boumedienne. These powerful images give us a 20th-century example of the way we have come to see the rulers of the past, especially those of the Greek and Roman Empires. These are the modern portrayal of might and dominance.

DISCUSSION POINTS

● This head looks at us with eyes we cannot see. How can we tell what he is thinking? Eyes tell us so much; facial expressions help us to know whether other people are friendly or not. Eye contact is important as a means of communication. Sunglasses and visors deny us this opportunity to make eye contact. Many people use sunglasses to protect their eyes; visors protect eyes from damage when doing dangerous jobs. Do you think some people choose to hide behind these shields? Are they hiding from us? How do you feel when you wear sunglasses? What do you think about fashion in sunglasses? Are there sunglasses you would wear and some you wouldn't? Why is this?

● Where do you most often see people with their eyes covered? Think about motorcyclists, speedway riders and racing drivers. What sort of an image do these people have? Are they exciting, mysterious or threatening?

● This head is large. Try measuring your own heads. See how much they vary in size and shape. Compare the size of your heads with this one made of bronze. Why do you think the sculptor has made it this size?

● What senses do you have which are centred in your head? (In addition to sight, hearing and taste we have balance and our brains.) How do you think you might change as you grow up? Will you feel and behave differently? What will you look like in a few years' time? What would you like to look like?

ACTIVITIES

● Using oil pastels or wax crayons and grey or buff sugar paper, make some life-size drawings of each other wearing sunglasses. To do this they will need to measure again carefully to make sure they make the drawing large enough. Ask the children to look carefully to see how much of the face is covered up and how much they can still see clearly. First, they should practise making the colours they can see on a spare piece of paper of the same colour. Make sure they are using the pastels or crayons thickly enough to cover the paper.

Key Stage 2
1(i), 1(iv), 1(v)

● See if you can get hold of a motorcycle helmet and a cyclist's helmet. Compare the two. Why are they different? Does a motorcyclist need more protection? Accidents occur to both sorts of riders and often when they are in collision with cars. Using these helmets as models, the children could make one or more drawings of them. Then choose the one they find most interesting or exciting and make a detailed coloured drawing or painting.

Key Stage 2
1(i), 1(iv), 1(v)

● With the knowledge they have gained from looking at these helmets, they could design one of their own for a specific activity. Talk about all the activities they do which could be hazardous or end up with an injury. It should be possible to design a helmet to fit which is light enough to be comfortable but effective in the activity they have chosen. The children could go on to make the helmet either in

Key Stage 2
1(iv), 1(x)

paper and card as a prototype or you could make a model of it in 'Modroc' (plaster bandage).

● Also using 'Modroc', they could make their own version of a 'Goggle Head'. Dame Elisabeth Frink uses plaster in her work.

EVALUATION

● Have the children understood how we can change our image by wearing different things?

● Have they been able to relate this to the way that some world leaders of today present themselves?

● Did they find out more about their own and other children's heads and appreciate the vulnerability of people in certain situations?

SUPPORTING INFORMATION

Resources:
– sunglasses
– goggles
– visors and helmets

Materials:
cardboard; wires; Modroc

Topics:
protection; disguise

Other works by the artist:
'Harbinger Bird III' (Collection of Alexander Bernstein)
'Spinning Man' (collection of the artist)

Comparisons:
'Study for Mlle Polagny' by Constantin Brancusi (Tate Gallery, London)
'Cyclops' by Eduardo Paolozzi (Tate Gallery)
'Helmet Head' by Henry Moore
'The Rout of San Romano' by Paolo Uccello (National Gallery, London) [card 21]

Bibliography:
Robertson, B, *Elisabeth Frink, Sculpture* (Deutsch)

19 'Mr and Mrs Andrews',
1748−49
Thomas Gainsborough
(1727−88)

(Oil on canvas, 70 cm × 119 cm)

National Gallery, London

ABOUT THE ARTIST

Thomas Gainsborough was born in Suffolk. His boyhood in the country-side gave him a great love of the English landscape. This is evident in this painting, which he made at the age of 21 and which is as much a landscape painting as a portrait.

Gainsborough was a natural painter and was famous for his brilliant technique. This can be seen in the way in which he describes the subtle colours of the landscape, the sky and the shimmering material of Mrs Andrews' dress in this painting.

Because he was so successful at an early age, he was in great demand as a portrait painter. It was very fashionable in the 18th century to have your portrait painted to 'show off' your wealth and possessions. Gainsborough lived in London and Bath and during his life made portraits of the wealthy and the famous.

In his studio, and for himself, he made little models of landscapes from vegetables, plants and minerals. He lit them by candlelight and drew and painted them for the pleasures they gave him. When he died, a wealthy and successful man, his house was full of unsold landscape paintings.

ABOUT THIS WORK

Like David Hockney's 'Mr and Mrs Clark and Percy' (card 12), this is a 'double portrait'. Mr and Mrs Andrews would have 'commissioned' Thomas Gainsborough to make this painting. They would have agreed upon a price in advance and the artist would have visited them at their house and estate and made studies of them in their favourite clothes. He would discuss with them possible settings for the portrait and make drawings of these. Then, when they had agreed upon the design for the painting, Gainsborough would make the painting in his studio. It was also commonplace for the sitter to visit the studio to view the painting in progress and to suggest changes and improvements!

Whereas David Hockney chose to paint his friends, Ossie and Celia Clark, Thomas Gainsborough was painting Mr and Mrs Andrews to order. In the 18th century, a successful portrait painter had to be able to please and flatter his clients as well as describe them and their possessions with great skill.

There were hundreds of portrait painters working in Britain in the 18th and 19th centuries. Today there are comparatively few because people can use photography to record each other, their possessions and their pastimes.

DISCUSSION POINTS

● Compare the way that the figures are posed in this painting with Mr and Mrs Clark in David Hockney's painting (card 12). How would you choose to pose for a painting or a photograph to look at your best?

● Look at other portrait paintings and at photographs of famous and fashionable people in magazines. Compare these with family photographs or newspaper photographs of people. Can you make a list of different methods used by painters or photographers to make people look more attractive and exciting than they really are?

● What can you tell about Mr and Mrs Andrews by looking at this painting? Imagine one of them to be a character in a book or film and describe what kind of person they are.

ACTIVITIES

Key Stage 2
1(i), 1(v)

● This painting is full of interesting detail. Using a viewfinder, ask the children to find part of the work that they particularly like. Make a careful and detailed drawing of the part they have chosen.

Key Stage 2
1(i), 1(viii)

● Gainsborough is famous for his ability to describe different kinds of surfaces with paint. Make two or three studies to compare different surfaces in the painting, e.g. bark of the tree, Mrs Andrews' dress, the dog's coat etc.

Key Stage 2
1(i), 1(vii)

● Look at all the different greens the artist has used in the landscape, or all the blues and greys in the clouds. Using pastels on a grey background, make a colour chart of the colours the children can see.

Key Stage 2
1(i), 1(iv), 1(x)

● Like Gainsborough, make a model landscape on a table using natural forms – leaves, bark, stones, sand etc. People it with toy farmyard animals and figures.

● Make three or four small drawings of different parts of the landscape. Ask the children to choose the one they like best and make a small painting from it using watercolours.

EVALUATION

● Have the children appreciated the great technical skill that Gainsborough brought to his paintings?

● Do they understand what it must have been like being an artist working to commission and how this compares with making paintings of your own choice?

● Can they recognise how painters and photographers use special methods and techniques to flatter and make as glamorous as possible the people who pose for them?

SUPPORTING INFORMATION

Resources:
– photographs of famous and fashionable people
– family photographs
– natural forms: leaves, bark, stones, plants etc. to make artificial landscapes

Topics:
families; dress

Other works by the artist:
'The Painter's Daughter' (National Gallery, London)
'The Market Cart' (Tate Gallery, London)

Comparisons:
'Mr and Mrs Clark and Percy' by David Hockney (Tate Gallery) [card 12]
'The Marriage of Giovanni Arnolfini' by Jan van Eyck (National Gallery, London)
'The Ambassadors' by Hans Holbein the Younger (National Gallery)

Bibliography:
Clark, *Landscape into art* (Pelican)
Gaunt, W, *A Concise History of English Painting* (Thames & Hudson)

20 'A Corner of the Artist's Room', 1907–09 Gwen John (1876–1939)

(31.7 cm × 26.7 cm)

Graves Art Gallery, Sheffield

ABOUT THE ARTIST

Gwen John was born in Haverfordwest in Wales. She had one sister and two brothers, one of whom, Augustus, studied with her and also became a painter. They went to the Slade School of Fine Art in London and then to Paris. Here Gwen joined the school run by J McNeill Whistler. She spent most of the rest of her life living and working near Paris. She earned her living in the early years by modelling for other women artists and for the famous sculptor Rodin. As she became better known, she was able to sell some of her paintings to an American collector in return for an annual allowance which enabled her to spend the rest of her years concentrating on her painting.

She painted many portraits of herself, her sister and several of her friends. She also painted interiors like the one we are looking at as well as landscapes, and she made many beautiful watercolours of the cats who were her constant companions.

ABOUT THIS PAINTING

Gwen John has chosen what appears to be a very plain and simple corner of her room to paint. The shapes and forms of the table, vase of flowers and the chair are so plain we could be tempted to think it over simplified and an easy picture to paint.

In reality, she has used enormous skill in handling paint to show us the subtle changes in light as it filters through the curtains into the room. Tones create the space within the picture and give us the feeling of tranquility, order and calm.

DISCUSSION POINTS

● This is a simple scene. It is the simplicity of the composition which makes it so interesting. When you paint a picture do you choose subjects as simple as this or do you prefer to show a scene full of objects? Look round the classroom. Has it got quiet areas which may give a feeling of peace? Do you have favourite corners or areas at home where you lie, or sit and read, or play?

● What patterns can you see in the picture? Some are obvious, such as the basket work of the chair and the wallpaper pattern; others are less easy to see, such as the tiles on the floor and the lace curtain at the window. Look round the room for patterns. See how many you can find. Are they patterns which are created by the way things were made or are they created by light and shade?

● Look carefully at the surface of the painting. Can you see the brush strokes? Are they long or short? When you are painting do you think about how you put the paint on to the paper? What difference does it make if you use thick or thin paintbrushes? What difference does it make if you see long or short brush strokes?

● Look at the shadows in the picture. Now look at shadows falling in the classroom. Do the colours change from light tones to darker ones? How can you achieve this when you are mixing paint? What is needed to make the paint darker in tone? Sometimes a shadow will just be a deeper tone of the same colour and sometimes it actually seems to change the colour to another shade. Can you see examples of this in the room?

ACTIVITIES

● You could simply use this picture as a way into looking at and making a painting of a small corner of your room or you could use any of the following ideas as single activities. However, they have also been planned in this instance to build together into a series of related pieces leading step by step to a finished painting.

Key Stage 2
1(i), 1(v)

● Begin by making a simple colour chart. Ask the children to begin with the lighter colours and test them out in small patches, building up swatches of colours to match each range of colours within the picture. They will need to work on coloured sugar paper as there is so much white in the painting.

Key Stage 2
1(vii)

● Using viewfinders, ask the children to look around the room and find three small areas to draw. Then choose the one they like best and make a slightly larger drawing of it in colour, using oil pastels or coloured pencils. Keep to a small, simple area of the room and one which is as uncomplicated as our example.

Key Stage 2
1(i), 1(v)

● The actual size of this picture is only slightly larger than A4 so that would be the best size to work on for these paintings. Using the coloured sketch for reference, begin work by painting in the background with pale tones of the colours that are there. Remember

Key Stage 2
1(i), 1(v), 1(vi),
1(vii), 1(viii)

about the brush strokes; take care not to make them too large and think about which direction they should go in. The children can always refer to the picture for guidance. Concentrate on getting the background tones right and then paint in the objects in the foreground.

EVALUATION

● Tone is a term used to describe the lightness or darkness of a colour. Did the children learn more about tones and how to make them from their paint by adding white, black or grey to the colour?

● Were the children able to understand how to make different sizes of brush marks and to control their direction?

SUPPORTING INFORMATION

Topics:
homes; colour and light

Other works by the artist:
'Mere Poupessin' (National Museum of Wales, Cardiff)
'Miss C Broughton Lewis' (Tate Gallery, London)
'Young Woman in a Red Shawl' (York City Art Gallery)
'The Convalescent' (private collection)

Comparisons:
'Interior with Table' by Vanessa Bell (Tate Gallery) [card 22]
'The Bowl of Milk' by Pierre Bonnard (Tate Gallery)
'Pot of Flowers in the Studio' by Edouard Vuillard (Scottish National Gallery of Modern Art, Edinburgh)

Bibliography:
Taubman, M, *Gwen John* (Wildwood House)

21 'The Rout of San Romano', circa 1450
Paolo Uccello (1397–1475)

(Wooden panel, 181 cm × 320 cm)

The National Gallery, London

ABOUT THE ARTIST

Paolo Uccello was born in Florence in 1397. Very little is known about his life apart from his work. At the age of ten he was apprenticed to the sculptor Ghiberti as an errand boy. In Ghiberti's workshops he trained to be a goldsmith and also learnt how to design and make mosaics and stained glass windows. An apprentice artist would work as an assistant to the master artist or craftsman until he had enough skills and reputation to set up his own studios and workshops.

The city-state of Florence in Italy was the birthplace of the **Renaissance** in the 15th century. Here, scientists, artists and philosophers began to challenge the dominance of the Catholic Church over all aspects of life and thought. Artists like Uccello began to base their work on the laws of science and mathematics, rather than to the rules laid down by the Church. Uccello was so inspired by the discovery of the mathematical rules of perspective that he spent an enormous amount of time practising and perfecting them to use in his paintings and **frescos**.

Uccello was an important painter because he pioneered ways of describing space scientifically and realistically in his work.

ABOUT THIS WORK

'The Rout of San Romano' is one of three panels of a triptych (a painting in three parts) which Uccello was commissioned to make to celebrate a victory by the Florentines over the neighbouring city-state of Siena. The triptych was made for the Medici Palace in Florence. This is the left-hand panel, showing the Florentine soldiers charging at their enemies. The other two panels are now in the Louvre in Paris and the Uffizi Gallery in Florence.

The Florentine army is led by Nicolo Mauricci da Tolentino. He is mounted on the white horse in the centre of the painting. Because he is the most important person in the painting he wears a red turban instead of a helmet so that his face can be seen and recognised. The battle is in full cry. All the important characters are in the foreground. In the background are foot soldiers fighting and other soldiers fleeing from the battle across the fields.

In the foreground you can see how Uccello has applied the rules of perspective (that all lines in the painting lead to a vanishing point). He has carefully placed the wounded soldier and the broken armour and lances so that they lead your eye to the centre of the painting.

In order to make this painting, the artist would have used people as models in his studio. He would have made preliminary studies and drawings of the figures before he 'composed' the painting. Even the horses were carefully posed and held in place with scaffolding and ropes while Uccello made drawings of what they would look like in battle.

DISCUSSION POINTS

● In the foreground, the artist has applied the rules of perspective (all lines in the painting lead to a vanishing point). Can you find the vanishing point for the foreground of the painting by following the lines of the broken lances on the ground? (The children can trace the lines on the card with fingers.)

● Where is the vanishing point for the landscape in the background of the painting?

● Compare the way that Uccello has explained distance in this picture by making the figures in the background much smaller than those in the foreground with the way that L S Lowry does this in his painting 'VE Day 1945' (card 9).

● Can you see how Uccello has made the scene more exciting and dramatic? He has placed the white and cream shapes of the horses and lances against the dark shape of the hedge and contrasted the dark shapes of the broken and abandoned weapons and armour with the pale ground of the battlefield.

● Look at the pattern of the lances and swords from left to right in the painting. Can you see how carefully they are arranged to emphasise the direction of the charge by the Florentine soldiers upon their enemies from Siena?

ACTIVITIES

● In order to help the children understand what is meant by 'foreshortening' get them to undertake the following tasks:

   – Pose one child like the fallen soldier in the foreground of the painting. Ask them to lie on a large sheet of white paper and then draw round their outline with charcoal or with a black felt pen. Compare what the outline looks like on the ground with its appearance when it is held vertical.

- Pose a child lying face up on a table. Ask the children to compare what the child looks like when viewed from the feet end and the head end. Make drawings from either end.

- Give each child an A4 sheet of paper on a clipboard. Ask them to place the clipboard on their lap and observe their view of their own knees and feet from above. Make drawings of this view with biro or micro liner.

Key Stage 2
General requirements,
1(i), 1(v), 1(vi)

● Ask the children to make drawings of all the different helmets worn by the soldiers in this battle scene. Discuss and compare their differences and how effective they might be in protecting the soldiers against swords and lances. As the helmets are all in profile, the drawings could be 'scaled up' and redrawn on white card. Then they could be mounted to make a frieze of helmets for display.

Key Stage 2
1(i), 1(viii), 1(x)

● In conjunction with the study of protective helmets and their design related to the sculpture 'Goggle Head' by Dame Elisabeth Frink (card 18), the children could make comparative studies of the effectiveness of different kinds of helmets and headgear. For example, compare the helmets and armour worn by the soldiers in this painting with those used by soldiers in the First and Second World Wars and in contemporary warfare.

Key Stage 2
1(iv)

EVALUATION

● Have the children appreciated that Uccello was making these important discoveries about how to draw and paint things in space over 500 years ago and that contemporary artists like L S Lowry also use his discoveries?

● Can they find other paintings where artists have used the rules of perspective to explain space and distance in a painting?

● Have they appreciated how difficult it is to draw people from certain viewpoints?

SUPPORTING INFORMATION

Resources:
- pictures and photographs of soldiers wearing different kinds of helmets, armour and uniform
- motorcycle helmet
- protective headgear

Topics:
protection; war

Other works by the artist:

'St George and the Dragon' (National Gallery, London)

'Hunt by Night' (Ashmolean Museum, Oxford)

Comparisons:

'V E Day, 1945' by L S Lowry (Glasgow Art Gallery and Museum) [card 9]

'Akbar's Forces Beseiging Ranthanbhor Fort in 1568' by Anon (Mughal) (Victoria & Albert Museum, London)

'Troops Resting' by Christopher Nevinson (Imperial War Museum, London)

'Wounded Men Filling Water Bottles in a Stream' by Stanley Spencer (Sandham Memorial Chapel, Burghclere, Hampshire)

Bibliography:

Carli, E, *All the Paintings of Uccello* (Oldbourne)

Paolieri, A, *Paolo Uccello* (Scala/Riverside)

22 'Interior with table', 1921
Vanessa Bell (1879– 1961)

(54 cm × 64.1 cm)

The Tate Gallery, London

ABOUT THE ARTIST

Vanessa was born into a family with a strong tradition in the arts. Her father was a writer and critic and there were artists and writers in her mother's family. Of the four children the two daughters became best known: Vanessa for her painting and Virginia, the writer who married Leonard Woolf and together founded the Hogarth Press. With this background, it was accepted that the children would follow their own artistic interests and Vanessa had drawing lessons from childhood. She went on to an art school when she was 17 and then to the Royal Academy Schools for a time. Here she met many of her generation who reacted against the established order. She and her sister became members of the 'Bloomsbury' group, together with other artists, writers and economists many of whom had met as undergraduates at Cambridge. They were strongly influenced by other artists and craftsmen, particularly William Morris and the Post-Impressionists. They formed the Omega workshops in 1913 to influence contemporary design and later the Bell family moved to a house called 'Charleston' in East Sussex where they decorated the interior and designed their own fabrics and furniture. This house is now open to the public.

ABOUT THIS WORK

Vanessa was living at 'Charleston' when she painted this picture. In complete contrast to the Gwen John painting (card 20 in this collection), it is strongly painted with a dark foreground and bright light falling on the landscape. The sky is blue and this is reflected in the quality of light falling on and reflected in the objects in the room.

DISCUSSION POINTS

- This picture was painted with clear colours and shapes. The curves of the table legs and chair contrast with the straight lines of the window frame and these are echoed in the trees and landscape beyond. Do you think the artist arranged this and deliberately chose furniture with curves?

● This is a good example of a painting which shows objects and landscape in layers, one seen behind the other. The arrangement of light and dark colours also contrast, with many repeated in different parts of the picture. Can you find the patterns made by blues, reds, greens and browns? Pick out each colour in turn.

● Where do you think the light is coming from in this picture? As you would expect, most of it is coming from outside, lighting up the curtains, walls and window frame. But if you look carefully at the shadows you will see some that are cast from the table against the wall. What might make this happen?

● Look at the window frame. These are french doors which were popular in the 1920s. How are they different to the patio doors many houses have now?

● The landscape in this painting is simply painted with little detail – just light, shade and colour. Look at the view from your window. What can you see? Think of it in terms of colour and light, not a mass of tiny details.

ACTIVITIES

Key Stage 2
1(i), 1(vii), 1(viii)

● What sort of view do you have from your classroom window? If it has any kind of landscape or town scene you could ask the children to make a simple colour drawing or painting of it. Suggest they try half closing their eyes until they can just see the view but lose all the detail. It may take time for them to practise this. Using either oil pastels or powder colour on buff or grey sugar paper, make a picture of the view. Try to keep to shapes and colours and, for once, leave out the detail. To make it more like their own version of this painting they could cut a window frame out of dark sugar paper to match the one in your room and stick it over their picture.

Key Stage 2
1(i), 1(v)

● Look carefully at the window frame in the picture and compare it with one in the classroom. How thick are the frames? Do they have many layers of wood or metal? How is the glass set into the frame? Ask the children to use pencil and cartridge or charcoal and chalk with grey sugar paper to make a careful study of part of one of the window frames to show either how the glass is set into the wood or metal, or how it opens.

Key Stage 2
1(i), 1(ii), 1(iv), 1(vi)

● The chair in the painting seems to be made of curved wood. Ask the children to use crayons or oil pastels on light coloured sugar paper to make a careful copy of the part of the chair they can see. Then they can go on to draw the rest of it as they think it might look. Remember to begin in the corner of the paper to leave space for the rest of the chair. You could get some ideas for this by asking the children to look around school and at home to see how many different chairs they can find.

EVALUATION

● Were the children able to understand how a landscape could look so full of light and colour with so little detail in it?

● Did they learn new things about how windows are constructed and appreciate how carefully they have to look to see all that is there?

● Could they appreciate how long ago this artist lived and how different the world was then? At that time, women were encouraged to paint for a hobby and have other pastimes but were frowned upon for taking it too seriously.

SUPPORTING INFORMATION

Resource:
–   collection of different chairs

Topics:
colour and light; homes

Other works by the artist:
'A Conversation' (Courtauld Institute, London)
'Still Life on Corner of Mantelpiece' (Tate Gallery, London)
'Studland Beach' (Tate Gallery)

Comparisons:
'A Corner of the Artist's Room' by Gwen John (Sheffield City Art Galleries) [card 20]
'Open Window' by Raoul Dufy (Tate Gallery)
'Interior with a Violin case' by Henri Matisse (Museum of Modern Art, New York)
'The Window' by Pierre Bonnard (Tate Gallery)

Bibliography:
Naylor, G, *Bloomsbury* (Octagon Group/Amazon)

23 'Blue and Green Music', 1919
Georgia O'Keeffe (1887–1986)

(Oil on canvas, 48 cm × 58 cm)

Alfred Stieglitz Collection, The Art Institute of Chicago, USA

ABOUT THE ARTIST

Georgia O'Keeffe was born in Wisconsin in America. Her father was a farmer and her childhood was spent in the countryside among cornfields and under wide skies. Her mother arranged painting lessons for her when she was ten years old. By the time she was 12 she knew she wanted to be an artist. She trained at the Art Institute of Chicago and then at the Art Students League in New York.

It was an exciting and challenging time to be training to be an artist in America in the early part of this century. Artists and students were being influenced by the exhibition in New York of the work of such European artists as Van Gogh, Matisse, Rousseau and Picasso (whose work is also represented in this collection). They were influenced by the Post-Impressionists' use of colour and by Picasso's 'Cubist' paintings. Up until this time, American painting had been very traditional and mainly concerned with representing everyday life in America.

Georgia O'Keeffe was one of the first American artists to make paintings which were '**abstract**' – paintings about the enjoyment of shapes and colours. She made paintings of familiar things: flowers, landscapes and buildings. In her famous paintings of flowers she observed them in close up – 'a bee's eye view' – and their shapes and colours fill the canvas like strange and exotic landscapes.

Another artist wrote about her work: 'In her canvasses each colour almost regains the fun it must have felt when forming the first rainbow.'

After Georgia finished her training, she worked as a commercial artist and then as a teacher before her reputation was such that she could make her living as an artist. During the latter part of her life she moved to New Mexico where her work was influenced and inspired by the dramatic hills and the isolated and empty landscapes of that part of America.

Georgia O'Keeffe continued painting well into her eighties and achieved recognition as being the greatest American woman painter of the 20th century.

ABOUT THIS WORK

This is an abstract painting. It does not describe something the artist has seen It is a painting about shapes and colours that Georgia O'Keeffe has found in plants and in landscapes.

She wrote about this kind of work: 'I get this shape in my head and sometimes I know where it comes from and sometimes I don't!'

You can look at this painting and see or imagine all kinds of things the painting might represent.

Georgia O'Keeffe loved music and found that different kinds of music conjured up different kinds of images for her. In this painting she was trying to describe the shapes and colours that she 'saw' when she listened to music.

DISCUSSION POINTS

● What is this painting about? What does it remind you of? In groups, write down all the different things that you can see in this painting. Compare and discuss the various things that the different groups write down. What are the most common elements observed in the painting?

● Why is the painting called 'Blue and Green Music'? What kind of music or sounds are suggested by the painting?

● Compare this picture with 'Broadway Boogie-Woogie' by Piet Mondrian (card 24). They are very different. Are they about different kinds of music? Can you find words to describe the moods in each of these paintings?

● Using a range of percussion instruments, can you make some sounds that match these paintings?

ACTIVITIES

● Collect a range of natural forms with interesting patterns and surfaces; for example, driftwood, shells, bark, pebbles etc. Ask the children to use magnifying glasses to find interesting patterns within these and to make careful drawings of these patterns. They can work with biros or fibre tip pens on cartridge paper.

Key Stage 2
1(i), 1(vi), 1(vii)

● Compare the patterns they have found and drawn with those to be found in landscapes in the locality, in photographs of different kinds of landscapes and in the work by Van Gogh, Uccello, Bruegel and Gainsborough in this collection (see cards 13, 21, 6 and 19).

Key Stage 2
1(iv), 1(vi)

● Make up two or three miniature landscapes on tables in the classroom using a variety of natural and made forms. Ask the children to

Key Stage 2
1(i), 1(vi), 1(viii)

observe these through colour filters or cellophanes. Discuss how the mood or feel of the landscape alters as it changes colour.

Key Stage 2
1(iv), 1(v)

● Ask the children to make small paintings (not bigger than 20 cm × 15 cm) in watercolour or powder colour from these landscapes. Use viewfinders to select an interesting section of landscape. Focus on shapes and surfaces.

Key Stage 2
1(iv), 1(vii), 1(xii)

● After making studies for the landscape, discuss how colour might be used to give their picture a particular mood. Ask the children to make their paintings in two colours plus white. They will need to practise first to decide which two colours will best give their landscape the kind of mood they require.

EVALUATION

● Have the children understood that an artist can describe things s/he has seen just using colours and shapes?

● Can they find other 'abstract' paintings and explain what they might mean?

● Have they appreciated that an artist can use colour to convey a particular mood or feeling in a painting?

● Can they find other paintings in this collection where colour is used in this kind of way?

SUPPORTING INFORMATION

Resources
– natural forms: driftwood, bark, shells, pebbles etc.
– magnifying glasses
– photographs of local landscapes

Topic:
colour

Other works by the artist:
'The Mountain, New Mexico' (Whitney Museum of Modern Art, New York, USA)
'The White Calico Flower' (Whitney Museum of Modern Art)
'Red Canna' (University of Arizona Museum of Art, USA)

24 'Broadway Boogie-Woogie', 1942–43 Piet Mondrian (1872–1944)

(Oil on canvas, 127 cm × 127 cm)

The Museum of Modern Art, New York

ABOUT THE ARTIST

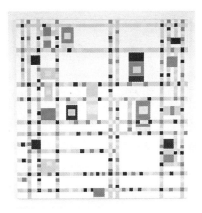

Piet Mondrian was born in Holland and began taking art lessons at the age of 14. When he was 19, he moved to Amsterdam where he trained as an artist.

He began work as a painter of flowers and landscapes. Like his contemporary, Henri Matisse, he was influenced by that group of artists called the 'Fauves' or 'Wild Beasts' who used dazzling colour in their work. In 1911 Mondrian moved to Paris where he was influenced by the work of the Cubists and their interest in seeking out the geometric structure of the natural world.

He was the first artist to make completely abstract paintings. By 1914/15 he was making paintings that consisted entirely of patterns of colour. He used only the three primary colours plus black, white and grey and horizontal and vertical lines.

In 1917 Mondrian founded a group called **De Stijl** ('The Style') which consisted of artists, architects and designers all committed to using simple geometrical shapes and colours in their work. They were reacting against the decorative and ornamental styles of building and design that were popular at the time. They wanted to replace it with work that was simple, pure and uncluttered.

Although Mondrian, through his own work, teaching and writing, had a great influence upon other artists and upon the design of buildings, furniture and fabrics, he was not a successful painter. He remained comparatively poor and unknown until he moved to America in 1938, for the last few years of his life. This painting, 'Broadway Boogie-Woogie', was his last work.

ABOUT THIS WORK

This is the most difficult painting to 'read' in this collection because Mondrian is not describing his experience of New York: he is placing together an arrangement of colours and shapes that he associates with the city – much as Georgia O'Keeffe was making colours and shapes that 'remind' you about landscapes in 'Blue and Green Music' (card 23).

The streets of New York are laid out in a geometrical pattern. Mondrian enjoyed looking down on the streets from the top of one of the many skyscraper buildings in the city. At night, he would have seen the blinking neon-light advertising signs and the stop-and-go traffic signs on every corner of the city and the constant stop–go flow of traffic. He would have seen all this against the constant background noise of 'boogie-woogie' music which was the 'pop' music of America in the 1940s.

Using only the three primary colours, plus white and grey, and working within a grid of horizontal and vertical lines, Mondrian has presented his 'view' of New York. It is a collection of shapes and colours that summon up for him the appearance and rhythm of city life.

DISCUSSION POINTS

● Compare this work with Georgia O'Keeffe's 'Blue and Green Music' (card 23). What are the most obvious differences between these two abstract works?

● Look at photographs of cities such as New York showing skyscrapers, aerial views, neon advertising signs etc. View any suitable video about city life at night. Listen to tapes of popular American music of the 1940s. (NB Glen Miller's music is easily available through re-recordings.) Ask the children to write about what they can 'see' in this painting after discussing the material about city life.

● Compare this work with paintings of cities by other artists, e.g. Canaletto, Utrillo, L S Lowry (card 9).

ACTIVITIES

Key Stage 2
1(i), 1(viii), 1(ix)

● Give the children a 30 × 30 centimetre square of white paper, a selection of different sized paper squares, rectangles in blue, red and yellow and thin strips of black paper. Ask them to try to make a simple and pleasing arrangement of shapes and colour within the white square. You can introduce such rules as 'use no more than five shapes' or 'no colour may be used more than twice' etc.

When they have made a satisfactory arrangement of one collection of shapes and colours, ask them to see how many other designs can be made with the same group of units. They can record these different designs on graph paper and with felt pens.

Key Stage 2
1(i), 1(iv)

● Collect visual evidence of your own city or a local city, e.g. photographs, maps, brochures, paintings. Ask the children to work in groups and within the group to make a collection of shapes, colours and surfaces that are characteristic of the city. They should look for common shapes of buildings, patterns within them, arrangements of buildings, road patterns, dominant colours within the city etc.

● Ask each group to make a collage, 75 × 75 centimetres, using a variety of papers and surfaces. It should describe for them the mood of the city.

Key Stage 2
I (viii)

   Use the collages as the basis for designing and making, within their groups, either a ceramic relief or a tapestry weaving about the city.

● Ask a small group of children to try to use the painting 'Broadway Boogie-Woogie' as a visual musical score. Can they decide within the group: Which colours represent which instruments? Whether the different shapes represent volume? How they might use the intervals between the squares to determine length of note? etc.

Key Stage 2
I (iv), I (v), I (vi)

   There is a rich variety of ways that the painting might be 'played'. Can they compose and play 'A city scene'?

EVALUATION

● Were the children able to appreciate that a painting doesn't have to be 'realistic' to describe what an artist has to say about his/her environment?

● Can they find other work where painters have similarly focused upon or emphasised particular colours or shapes to describe what they find to be important in the environment?

● Can they find photographs of buildings, furniture or fabrics in which architects and designers have used similar arrangements of shapes and colours to those used by Mondrian in his painting?

SUPPORTING INFORMATION

Resources:
– photographs of cities
– aerial views of cities
– American popular music e.g. Glen Miller
– percussion instruments
– local information through maps, photographs, guides, brochures etc.

Materials:
for paper collage – paper rectangles in red, blue and yellow; strips of black paper

Topics:
city life; musical rhythm

Other works by the artist:
'Composition' (National Museum of Modern Art, Paris, France)
'A Tree' (Munson Williams Proctor Institute, New York)

Comparisons:
'Blue and Green Music' by Georgia O'Keeffe (The Art Institute of
    Chicago, USA) [card 23]
'The Snail' by Henri Matisse (Tate Gallery, London)
'Swinging' by Wassily Kandisky (Tate Gallery)
'Painting 1937' by Ben Nicholson (Tate Gallery)

Bibliography:
Busignaric, A, *Mondrian* (Thames & Hudson)

Glossary

Abstract art

Art which does not imitate or directly attempt to represent external reality. It is non-figurative art. Underlying all abstract art is the idea that forms and colour in themselves can move the viewer. Examples of this style have been found in ceramic decorations, and in decorative patterns in manuscripts such as the Book of Kells. The original source of the painting, e.g. a *still life* or landscape, may be visible. Often abstract art includes simplified shapes which have no direct link with reality, as in Mondrian's work. In a third type of abstraction, brush-strokes, colour and textures of the material used suggest the development of the painting. Abstraction became more common in paintings and sculptures in the 1920s and has continued in various forms since.

Cézanne, Paul (1839–1906)

French painter who was given an allowance by his father at the age of 22, allowing him to paint without distraction for the next 23 years. He took part in the first Impressionist exhibitions of 1874 and 1877. Although he withdrew more and more from contact with others, his fame grew and he became a legendary figure in the art world. His later work involved a synthesis of reality and abstraction – showing the way for the development of *Cubism*.

Circa

Around a particular date, e.g. circa (or c.) 1400.

Cubists/Cubism

This *abstract* style of art was first named by an art critic after hearing a remark by Henri Matisse about the little cubes painted by Georges Braque. The first truly Cubist works are those in which objects, land-scapes and people are represented as many-sided solids. Cubism replaced *Fauvism* as the leading artistic movement in Paris around 1909 and has continued to have an important influence on art in the 20th century. Pablo Picasso and *Paul Cézanne* are two of the most notable Cubist exponents.

Der Blaue Reiter (German: 'The Blue Rider')

This group of German Expressionist painters was led by Marc, Kandinsky and Macke. The name was invented by Kandinsky, who had a passion for blue, and Marc who was keen on horses. They held two exhibitions in Munich in 1912 and 1913; the exhibitors included Picasso and Paul Klee. They placed an emphasis on child art as a source of inspiration, abstract forms and the symbolic and psychological aspects of line and colour. The group disbanded in 1914.

De Stijl

A group of artists, including the Dutch abstract painter, Piet Mondrian. The name came from a magazine. This group advocated the use of basic forms, particularly cubes, verticals and horizontals. De Stijl ideas influenced the *abstract art* of the 1930s.

frescos (meaning: fresh)

These are wall-paintings where the paint is spread on to a freshly plastered wall, often in churches.

Fauves/Fauvism

This is a style of *abstract art* in which flat patterns and free, bold handling of colour are the main themes. It was influenced by the work of Van Gogh. The name was first used in 1905 to describe a room at the Salon d'Automne in which a classical sculpture by Albert Marque was sur-rounded by paintings by Matisse, Darain and others. Fauvism gave way to *Cubism* after a few years.

Foreshortening

This term is applied in painting and drawing to where perspective is used to single objects or figures to create the illusion of projection and depth. It was first found on Greek vases (*circa* 500 BC) but was not developed until the *Renaissance*.

'genre' (French: type, kind)

In literary terms 'genre' means writing of a particular format and style, e.g. science fiction, mystery, thriller, romance. In art, it relates to a type of painting. It was first applied to paintings in the 17th century, when the life of ordinary people was depicted in Dutch art.

Hieroglyphics (Greek: sacred carving)

This mode of writing was used by the ancient Egyptians, and others. It consisted mainly of picture writing or syllables/letters. Sometimes a picture stands for a word or a notion; so the figure, device or sign can have a hidden meaning: e.g. a figure of a tree or an animal may stand for a word, a syllable or a sound.

Icons (Greek: image)

Religious paintings used as objects of worship. They often portray the Virgin and Child. Later Russian icons show a figure surrounded by a halo of precious metals and stones. An iconostasis is a church screen covered with icons placed between the congregation and the altar.

Impressionist

An artist from a major movement in art that spread throughout Europe from the late 1890s. The term comes from Monet's painting 'Impression Sunrise' (1874) and became a label for the group of artists who ex-hibited as the 'Society of Painters, Etchers and Engravers'. They aimed to capture a scene (usually landscape) as a visual impression and not as a 'factual' report. They concentrated on the play of light on the scene. An Impressionist painting is a sketch, as opposed to a finished picture.

Miniatures

As the name suggests, these are minute paintings. The term originally applied to the art of manuscript illumination but was later used of paintings executed on a very small scale. They are usually portraits. In the 16th century miniaturists painted using gouache on vellum or card. By the 18th century it had become usual to paint in transparent watercolour on ivory. This art style had begun to decline by the mid-19th century.

Post-Impressionists

This was a term first used to describe the artists exhibiting in London in 1910 – including *Cézanne*, Matisse, Picasso and Van Gogh. It does not imply a similarity of style, although all the artists were reacting against the *Impressionist* preoccupation with visual appearances.

Pre-Raphaelite Brotherhood

This was a group of seven young English painters and sculptors formed in 1840: W Rossetti, Dante Rossetti, John Everett Millais, J Collinson, F Stephens, T Woolner and W H Hunt. They wished to revive purity of art and hoped to achieve this by choosing simple subjects and using clarity of colour and line. The movement affected other painters, such as Ford Maddox Brown. Their realistic treatment of Biblical subjects provoked much indignation.

Primitive painters

Name given to artists, usually self-taught, whose technique is by academic standards clumsy and whose work is sometimes naive in approach and vision. The term 'primitive art' refers to the art of primitive peoples and should be distinguished from work by 'primitive painters'. Primitive art from Africa and Oceania influenced western painting and sculpture in the early 20th century (see *Cubism*).

Renaissance

This was a cultural and artistic revolution which originated in city-states in northern Italy in the 14th century, before spreading through Europe. The Church and wealthy nobles, such as Lorenzo de' Medici, were patrons (sponsors) of the arts. Artists were elevated to a position of inspired creators. Renowned Renaissance artists include Donatello, Leonardo da Vinci, Botticelli, Michaelangelo and Raphael. The human figure became the most important part of their artwork. By paying special attention to human anatomy and applying the laws of perspective, the artists produced figures that were expressive in movement and gesture and depicted the dignity of men and women.

Sienese school (or school of Siena)

Italian painting which flourished in Siena, Italy, in the 13th to 15th centuries. It was more conservative than other *Renaissance* art, being inclined towards decorative beauty and the elegant grace of late Gothic art.

Still life

Inanimate objects, e.g. flowers, fruit, dead game, vessels etc., are represented in painting/drawing.

TIME LINE OF ARTISTS' WORK IN RESOURCES PACK

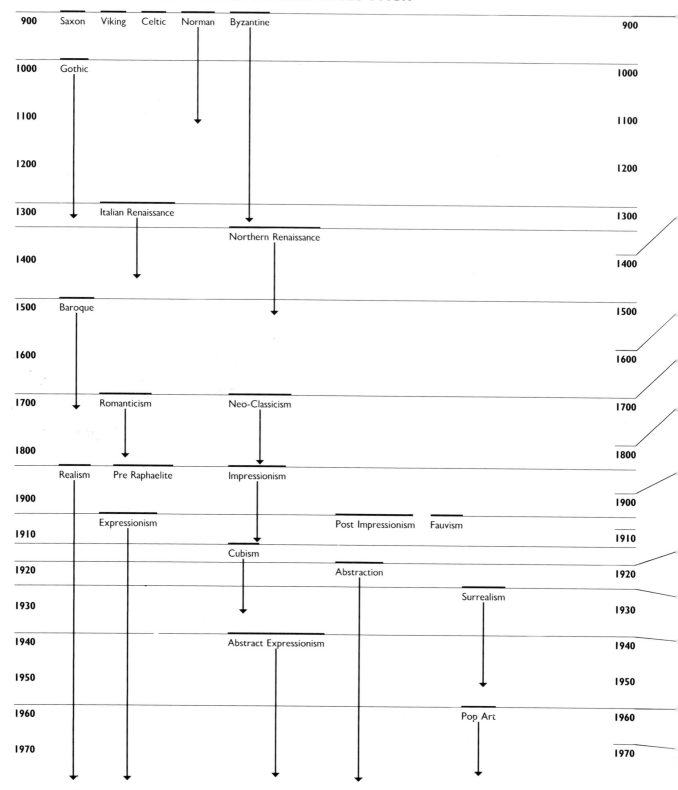

| 900 | Saxon | Viking | Celtic | Norman | Byzantine | | 900 |

1000 — Gothic

1100

1200

1300 — Italian Renaissance — Northern Renaissance

1400

1500 — Baroque

1600

1700 — Romanticism — Neo-Classicism

1800

Realism — Pre Raphaelite — Impressionism

1900

1910 — Expressionism — Post Impressionism — Fauvism

Cubism

1920 — Abstraction

1930 — Surrealism

1940 — Abstract Expressionism

1950

1960 — Pop Art

1970

Date	No	Title	Period/Country	Links
900 AD	17	The Book of Kells	Celtic	Saxon Viking Norman
1450	21	Paolo Ucello 'The Rout of San Romano'	Italian Renaissance	
1556	6	Pieter Bruegel 'The Census at Bethlehem'	Northern Renaissance	
1556	3	British School 'The Cholmondeley Sisters	Tudor	
1600 c.	8	Yoruba 'Carved wooden gates'	Africa (Benin)	
1630	5	Abu'l Hassan 'Twelve Squirrels in a Chennar Tree'	India (Mughal Empire)	
1749	19	Thomas Gainsborough 'Mr and Mrs Andrews'	Neo-Classical	
1750	14	Torii Kiyohiro 'The Spinning Top'	Japan	
1855	15	Ford Maddox Brown 'The Last of England'	Pre-Raphaelite	Realism/Social comment
1884	11	John Everrett Millais 'Autumn Leaves'	Pre-Raphaelite	
1888	13	Vincent Van Gogh 'Landscape near Mont Majour'	Post Impressionist/Impressionist	
1891	1	Henri Rousseau 'Tropical Storm with Tiger'	Primitive	
1909	20	Gwen John 'A corner of the Artist's Room'	Post-Impressionist– Realist	
1911	7	Henri Matisse 'The Goldfish Bowl'	Post-Impressionist/Fauvism	
1919	23	Georgia O'Keefe 'Blue and Green Music'	Post Impressionist/Cubist/ Symbolist	
1921	22	Vanessa Bell 'Interior with a Table'	Bloomsbury Group/ Post Impressionist	
1922	4	Paul Klee 'A Girl's Adventure'	Cubist/Abstract/ symbolist/	
1925	10	Pablo Picasso 'Still Life with Fish'	Cubist/Expressionist	
1937	16	Stanley Spencer 'Southwold'	Post Impressionist/ Symbolist	
1943	24	Piet Mondrian 'Broadway Boogie–Woogie'	Abstract	
1945	9	L.S. Lowry 'V.E. Day'	Primitive/ Social realist	
1967	18	Dame Elizabeth Frink 'Goggle Head'	Expressionist	
1969	2	Leon Kossoff 'Children's Swimming Pool'	Abstract Expressionist	
1971	12	David Hockney 'Mr and Mrs Clark and Percy'	Pop Art	

General Bibliography

Baker, S, and Baker, N, *Masters of Art* (Galahad)

Bell, C, *The French Impressionsists* (Phaidon)

Clark, K, *Landscape Into Art* (Pelican)

Compton, S (ed.), *British Art in the Twentieth Century* (Prestel)

Cummings, R, *The Master Painter* series (Methuen)

Cummings, R, *Just Look* (Viking Kestrel)

Ehrlich, D, *Masterpieces of Twentieth Century Painting* (Brampton)

Ferrier, J, *Art of Our Time* (Prentice Hall)

Gaunt, W, *A Concise History of English Painting* (Thames & Hudson)

Gombrich, E, *The Story of Art* (Phaidon)

Harris, R, *Every Picture Tells a Story* (Phaidon)

House, J, *Impressionist Masterpieces* (Art Line Editions)

Januszczak, W, *Techniques of the World's Great Painters* (Tiger)

Johnson, H W, *The History of Art for Young People* (Thames & Hudson)

Knapp, H, *Enjoying Pictures* (Routledge Kegan & Paul)

Lloyd, C, *A Picture History of Art* (Phaidon)

Parris, L, *Landscape in Britain* (Tate Gallery Publications)

Pischel, G, *A World History of Art* (Guild Publishing)

Read, H, *A Concise History of Modern Sculpture* (Thames & Hudson)

Reynolds, G, *Victorian Painting* (Guild Publishing)

Richardson, W, *Cities Through the Eyes of Artists* (Macmillan)

Richardson, W, *Animals Through the Eyes of Artists* (Macmillan)

Rose, B, *American Art Since 1900* (Thames & Hudson)

Rothenstein, J, *The Tate Gallery* (Thames & Hudson)

Rowling, G, *Art Source Book* (Chartwell)

Shone, R, *The Century of Change* (Phaidon)

Sinclair and Baker, *Masters of Art* (Galahad)

Smith, A, *Painting and Painters* (Wayland)

Terrier, J-L, *Art of Our Century* (Prentice Hall)

Towell, J, *Painting and Sculpture* (Wayland)

Tucker, W, *The Language of Sculpture* (Thames & Hudson)

Ventura, P, *Great Painters* (Kingfisher)

Wilding, G, *Understanding Art – Faces*
                     – People at Work
                     – People at Home (Wayland)

Wood, C, *The Pre-Raphaelites* (Guild Publishing)

Woolf, F, *Picture This* (Hodder & Stoughton)